PAPAYA with SUGAR

ALICE EVES

First published 2016

Copyright © 2016 Marilyn Larthe

Marilyn Larthe has asserted her right under the Copyright, Designs and Patents Act, 1988 to be identified as the author of this work. All rights reserved. No unauthorised use.

Typeset in the UK.

This book is sold subject to the condition that it shall not, by way of trade or otherwise, be lent, resold, hired out, or otherwise circulated without the publisher's prior consent in any form of binding, cover other than that in which it is published and without similar condition including this condition being imposed on the subject purchaser.

ISBN 13: 978 1535 22 9906
ISBN 10: 1535 22 990 X

Book design by The Art of Communication www.book-design.co.uk
Images © Marilyn Larthe and Shutterstock
Watercolour of Sitka by Douglas Addison

SOUTH PACIFIC

To see a world in a grain of sand
And heaven in a wild flower,
Hold infinity in the palm of your hand
And eternity in an hour

(William Blake. 1757 – 1827)

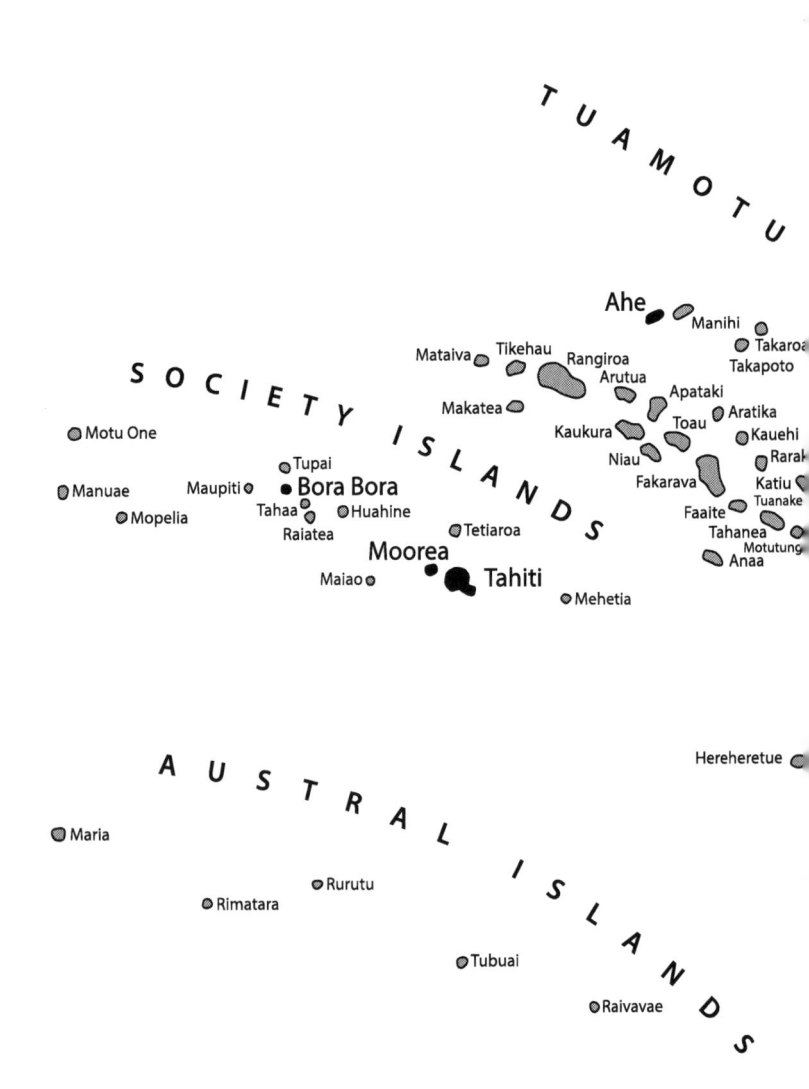

PAPAYA WITH SUGAR

SOUTH PACIFIC OCEAN

TUAMOTU

SOCIETY ISLANDS

Ahe
Manihi
Mataiva   Tikehau   Rangiroa
Takaroa
Arutua
Takapoto
Makatea
Apataki
Motu One
Kaukura   Toau   Aratika
Kauehi
Tupai
Niau
Rarak
Manuae   Maupiti   Bora Bora
Fakarava
Katiu
Mopelia
Tahaa   Huahine
Faaite   Tuanake
Raiatea   Tetiaroa
Tahanea
Moorea   Tahiti
Motutung
Maiao
Anaa
Mehetia

AUSTRAL ISLANDS

Hereheretue

Maria
Rurutu
Rimatara
Tubuai
Raivavae

ALICE EVES

MARQUESAS ISLANDS

- Hatutu
- Eiao
- Motu Iti
- **Nuku Hiva**
- Ua Huka
- **Ua Pou**
- Fatu Huku
- Tahuata
- Hiva Oa
- Motane
- Fatu Hiva

ARCHIPELAGO

- Tepoto
- Napuka
- Puka-Puka
- Tikei
- Taiaro
- Takume
- Fangatau
- Taenga
- Raroia
- Fakahina
- Makemo
- Hiti
- Nihiru
- Tepoto
- Marutea
- Tekokota
- Rekareka
- Tauere
- Tatakoto
- Haraiki
- Hikueru
- Amanu
- Reitoru
- Marokau
- Ravahere
- Hao
- Pukarua
- Nengonengo
- Paraoa
- Akiaki
- Reao
- Vahitahi
- Manuhangi
- Nukutavake
- Vairaatea
- Pinaki
- Ahunui

GAMBIER ISLANDS

- Anuanuraro
- Anuanurunga
- Nukutepipi
- Vanavana
- Tureia
- Tenararo
- Tenarunga
- Vahanga
- Tematangi
- Moruroa
- Matureivavao
- Marutea
- Fangataufa
- Maria
- Mangareva
- Morane
- Temoe

PAPAYA WITH SUGAR

Map of the Pacific Ocean showing California and some of the key countries in relation to the voyage route.

← Tokyo

PACIFIC OCEAN

The Pacific is the largest ocean. It is twice the size of the Atlantic.

Guam

HAWAII

SOLOMON ISLANDS

TAHITIAN ISLANDS

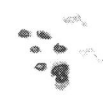

AUSTRALIA

NEW ZEALAND

ALICE EVES

Channel Islands Oxnard Los Angeles San Diego U.S.A.

Catalina Island

MEXICO

Equator — — — — — — — — — Galapagos Isles

MARQUESAS

TUAMOTU

Pitcairn Isle

Easter Isle

CHILE →

Valdivia →

PAPAYA WITH SUGAR

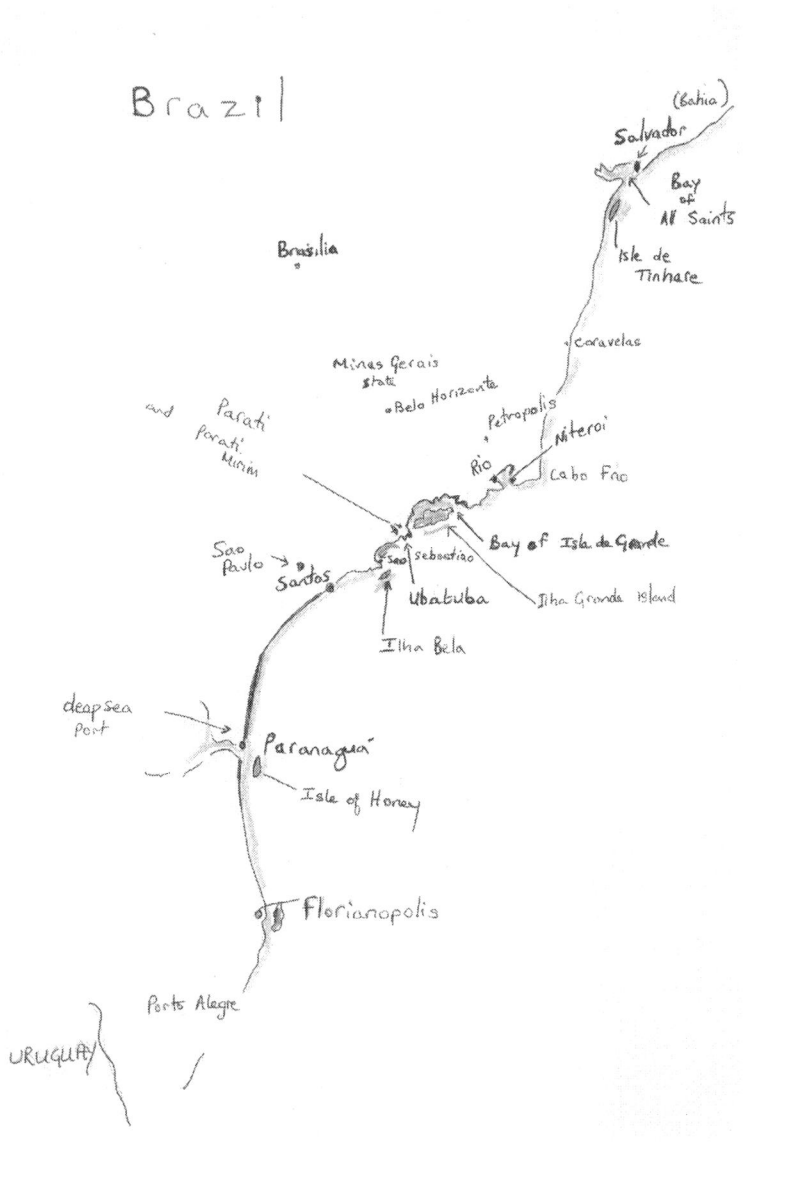

The maps are hand drawn sketches. They are not to scale and are simply to give an idea of the geographic relationship between the places visited. There are over 3,000 islands in Chile my drawing shows only a few.

ALICE EVES

Argentina and Chile showing the Strait of Magellan, the Beagle Channel and Cape Horn.

PAPAYA WITH SUGAR

Chapter One

Eleven o'clock in the morning, Oxnard, California. Sunday, 27th April. Today we began our adventure.

Our sailboat "Plainsong" was loaded to the gunnels with food and supplies. A thirty five foot ocean cruiser, a Tradewind designed by John Rock. We have filled her with food for three months and supplies of clothes, batteries and spare parts for a year and a half.

Oxnard is a commercial town just north of Los Angeles and south of Santa Barbara, where we have sailed Plainsong out of the Marina for the past five years.

Our friends arrived for a leaving party to wish Francis and I bon voyage bringing good will and strawberries, champagne, bagels, coffee cake and English scones. These were all cheerily shared and I think new friendships were made between our friends! Ignoring champagne for the first time, we kept to fruit juice.

It was a typical pleasantly hot Southern Californian day with a cloudless sky and a tiny breeze. Our friends clambered about the boat and pontoon wondering about our setting off on such a big adventure. They liked the idea but most were pleased it was not going to be them so far from land making ocean passages.

The party over we let the lines go attaching us to shore and set off. Some of our friends waved from the quay, others jumped aboard the boat of Ralph and Arnie, who had the berth next to us in Oxnard Marina, others on to the boat of Mike and Wendy and they all sailed with us for a mile beyond the breakwater.

It was a festive sight leaving the boats behind as our friends were hollering and shouting, waving and blowing kisses across the water. They are all dear friends and I would miss them. I wanted us all to sail together in the Marquesas, in the South Pacific. The Marquesas Islands are 6,200 km from California and 1,200 km north of Tahiti. Our friends stood on the boats with their baseball caps keeping the sun from their eyes, their white or bright tee shirts, their tidy shorts, their docksiders and wearing the biggest smiles, they waved as we disappeared.

The afternoon had been smooth with a calm sea as we sailed down towards Los Angeles and our destination, San Diego. We are sailing with an experienced sailor and friend Steve and will share the watches. At six o'clock I went below to prepare supper. After ten minutes I escaped on to the deck. Francis says I have a stomach of cast iron but it didn't feel like that then. The wind was blustery and a big swell was rolling us even though the wind was light. The sea got worse. The swell was confused and was coming from all directions.

We had entered the California eddy. It is wind and current streaming strongly from the north then being diverted this way and that by the Channel Islands which lie just off the coast between Los Angeles and Santa Barbara.

Feel slightly sick. I take a sea sickness pill. Perhaps too late because I continue feeling not so good for the next six hours. Francis had been encouraging me for the past two years that we had been planning this adventure to do the long sea passages with him. He wants me to do the voyages of a month with no land across the Pacific from San Diego to the Marquesas and later from Tahiti to Chile with a possible stop at Easter Island or Pitcairn and also the stormy sail around Cape Horn. I didn't like the idea of four or more weeks at sea with nowhere to land in a storm. I said I would do other parts of the journey with just a week of night passages with no land. This confused swell confirms my initial decision and I decide that I will not do the journey with Francis and our friend, Murray, sailing from San Diego to the Marquesas but will do the nine hundred miles Marquesas to the Tahitian Islands.

I do the midnight to two thirty night watch. There are no vessels sighted.

It can be eerie doing a night watch. The squeaking of the wind vane and the squawking of the self steering equipment and the ropes around them tightening and rubbing as the boat moves along in the darkness seem so much louder than in the day when one hardly notices these sounds at all.

The darkness seems filled with voices from the dark, deep sea. I look out there is no-one there. No visible sea birds or seals. I realize it is the equipment but I also realize what the sailors of old thought. Alone on deck it is easy to think of mermaids, of sailors and passengers lost at sea forever calling to be saved and taken ashore. I shiver.

Above the stars are glistening. Orion's Belt, the Great Bear or Big Dipper, Leo and the Little Bear make our life, our human life, on earth seem such a transient experience, such a short duration, a blink of the eye in the majesty of time.

I see a shooting star. It falls almost to the sea then disappears. I imagine Father Time wandering about the heavens at night with a small sack and collecting all the shooting stars as they fall.

The moon, that had been shrouded by cloud, appears and lights up the sky, throwing a pathway in front of us down which we travel. It is cold here under the moon yet magical.

Off watch I enjoy a sound sleep and feel much better.

5.10 p.m. The following day. We have now left Santa Catalina Island behind after sailing beside her all day. Catalina, measuring 22 miles by 7 miles, is the only permanently inhabited California Channel Island. There is a small town, Avalon, facing the mainland, and then behind it on the other side of the island, at the narrowest part, is Two Harbours, just a small bay but open to the ocean. 88% of the island is run by a non-profit conservancy. Catalina has pretty architecture with good cafes, restaurants and hotels. My favourite romantic hotel is The Inn at Mount Ada, high on a hill overlooking the bay. The house once belonged to Mr Wrigley of chewing gum fame. With only six double bedrooms it feels more like

Plainsong

staying as a guest in a beautiful home than being in a hotel. Catalina is across the water from Los Angeles and there is a ferry from Long Beach if you don't go by private boat. We have sailed into the bay at Avalon many times. This time we sail by until gradually it is simply a smudge below the sky.

Boat speed varied between 3 knots in the morning to six knots in the late afternoon. Wind strength has picked up slightly and is now a pleasant twelve knots. We are sailing with just the main and the colourful drifter up. The drifter is a lighter sail than a spinnaker and is excellent when sailing in light airs.

Francis and Steve take an afternoon nap because they are doing most of the night watches and I do a large chunk during the day. We expect to arrive in San Diego tomorrow afternoon. It will have taken us about fifty three hours non-stop sailing if we arrive at about four thirty on Tuesday.

I hope the sea has less swell tonight. People say when you are on watch you just glance around every quarter of an hour, but that is not quite true when a swell is running. A large swell prevents you seeing more than a few yards until it rolls underneath you. In that gap before the next swell rises, then is the time you look around for other vessels or navigation lights. So you must look out attentively because the other vessel might not be looking with a physical look out or at their radar. For instance last night in the dark before the moon appeared, a light flashed four times. It had a ten second interval. So a glance away for a minute in the interval would have missed the light on the buoy warning you of a rock just below the sea.

San Diego, Tuesday

Arrive at Point Loma close to dawn. At six am we round the point and there are six sailboats heading out from San Diego towards Los Angeles. They may be returning from the Newport Beach to Ensenada, Mexico race.

By half nine in the morning we find a berth at the Cabrillo Isle Marina, seven hours earlier than we anticipated. It has taken forty six hours. The wind today was light with some sun.

Plainsong moored in the Marquesas

Chapter Two

7th May I flew to England to find a house to buy to have somewhere to live when we finish the adventure. Steve goes back home to the Valley in Los Angeles. Murray flew in from England a couple of days before and has settled in nicely. Francis and his good and old friend, Murray, set off at lunch time for the Marquesas.

I met up with my parents in England and my father drove us to a village near Brighton where we stayed with Murray's wife Judith. Judith, a general practitioner, is a dear friend of mine. Judith and her children made us all welcome and fed us a hot, delicious dinner. After that, while we all slept, Judith had to complete five patient visits during the night.

30th May. Today I should have flown to the Marquesas but good news arrived in the post. I've passed the California Bar Exam! Fortuitously the oath admittance ceremony is in four days time so I have changed my flight from LA.

Tuesday, 3rd June. I borrowed some shoes from a friend to wear at the ceremony because all I had was a pair of sailing sandals. I did have one decent dress with me to wear and I was ready. It gave me a feeling of relief to have passed and I was happy because I wanted to specialize in business and commercial law, which to me is fun and stimulating and is as much fun as dancing – it is dancing for the brain.

Four California Judges made short, welcoming speeches directing us to be truthful and not to be in law for the money. I fear much of what they said may have fallen on deaf ears. After several Judges told us how clever we were, a female Judge brought us back to earth with a joke.

Amazingly, I receive a phone message from the LA City Attorney's Office about leading the County wide mediation project. For some time I'd been enjoying time as a volunteer there and this was the opportunity of a lifetime. It was for me a perfect job: no it was more than that, it was a vocation, it was work with meaning. It was some of the best work I would ever do. The people in the City Attorney's Office were bright and intelligent with kind hearts. It was a hard thing to have to do, but I had to say no. I had already started this sailing adventure, after which I was moving back to England. This was a different opportunity of a lifetime,

6th June. Left for the South Pacific after a few days obtaining more boat supplies.

Polynesian woman wearing tomato necklace at the airport, Papeete

Chapter Three

I arrived in Papeete, Tahiti in the Society Islands at a quarter to three in the morning. Four muscians played gentle Polynesian rhythms in the small airport arrival area. A travel company had been arranged to meet me and take me to my hotel. A smiling female guide met me and placed a garland, or lei, over my shoulders of fragrant gardenia flowers. I and my bags were whisked off into the dark, moist night to my hotel only five minutes away. I was both tired and happy after a comfortable eight and a half hour Air New Zealand flight. At the hotel I was greeted by a member of staff who gave me a tall, cool glass of mango juice. A delightful welcome. I was already thinking this was a great place.

I woke to a sunny, warm day with a stunning view from my room. There were gardens with exotic flowers; lush, green mountains; tall, thin, curved palm trees and a turquoise lagoon.

I had a one day lay over before my flight the next day at six am. Pottered about near the hotel recovering from the flight and being awake for thirty hours. As I walked in the garden, or along the beach, or sat having lunch it seemed odd hearing French all around so far from France. I supposed it must be no odder to the French when they travel and hear English spoken so far from England.

Woke at four am, left the hotel at five am and the plane left at six am for Nuka Hiva, the Marquesas Islands. It was an ATR 42 propeller plane and was just about full. Almost all passengers were Polynesian. It was a smooth flight of three and a half hours over almost empty ocean. We flew over a long, long, thin sandy looking finger of land that I think may have been Rangiroa in the Tuamotus.

Next to me sat a wonderful Polynesian who ran her own business in the Marquesas, a bed and breakfast and also made hats and mats from pandanus and palm tree leaves. Around her neck was a beautiful necklace of large, bright red beads. I expressed my admiration. She told me the beads were tomatoes! I looked closely – they were.

The pilot avoided flying through the thick, high towers of clouds that rose from other clouds though we passed

Our supply of bananas

close to them. Coming in to land I could see the dark green island. Then we were speeding over a hilltop. I thought that we would land down on the ground as happened in Tahiti. But no, all of a sudden the hill and the plane rushed at each other and it was to be a top of the hill landing. We came to a sudden stop. Silence. We emerged into a strange and beautiful land.

Francis was there to meet me. He looked healthy, tanned and happy. We shared a four wheel drive taxi with another couple and began the two and a quarter hour journey down the mountain to the village of Taihoae. A journey of only 12 miles as the crow flies. Francis knew I'd dislike the journey because the road was perilous. The Land Rover clung to the edge of the road where the land fell away precipitously hundreds of feet.

It was unpaved, just rough muddy track all the way. We ploughed through troughs of water and squelchy mud, through low cloud and looked over ridges giving views of dairy farms down on the plateau. Halfway down we got a good view of the bay and could see Plainsong bobbing gently in the water.

Coconut trees fringed the small bay and grew in clumps up the mountainside along with frangipani, bougainvillea, gardenia and breadfruit trees. As we drove along the air was fragrant with ylang-ylang and vanilla.

Several times we stopped to look at the view. On the last occasion the man of the couple in the taxi took his normal place in the back seat of the vehicle next to Francis and I. His wife sat in the front. Suddenly the man began shouting, not very loud but urgently. His wife had trapped three of his fingers in the door when she slammed it shut. Because it was a hot day he had his hand out of the window resting on the side of the car. It took her maybe ten seconds to realize what had happened but it felt a very long time. Luckily once the door was opened and his hand moved only one finger was bleeding. It was still attached and not as bad as I'd feared. It was bloody, blue and sore. We were now only twenty minutes from their small hotel where he would be able to get treatment.

Taiohae Bay, on Nuka Hiva island is 8 degrees below the equator. The only transport on the island is by four wheel drive vehicles, of which there are few, or by horse, of which there are many. Chestnut horses are tethered here and there as people work. Small motor boats are used to get around to the different bays of the island because the mountainous interior makes it difficult to cross. All the men had tattoos.

Two men were in the sea washing their horses. Other men were laying out coconut pieces on racks to dry. Each tattooed man had a flower behind his ear. There is a Catholic church with fine carved entrance doors and statues from local wood. The statues are of strong men conveying their warrior heritage which existed from time immemorial until the early 1900s. The stone of the church came from this and other nearby islands.

At a small shop we bought pamplemousse, the large, thick-skinned grapefruit, and onions. The shelves were more empty than full. There were several jars of mayonnaise so that distributor does a good job getting the product to distant ocean islands. The women in the shop and those we passed on the track had yellow hibiscus in their hair.

There are fifteen boats in the bay all, like us, doing a Pacific journey from the USA. Most of them belong to New Zealanders or Austrialians. Ours is the only English one.

The local name for these Marquesas Islands is Te Henua Enana, "Land of Men". They are 4,000 km south of Hawaii and 1,400 km north east of Tahiti. Nuka Hiva is the largest island in the group and is the administrative capital. It has a population of 7,500.

Polynesia is the land where Captain Bligh had a mutiny on his hands as the men grabbed at the chance to wed or otherwise stay with Polynesian women. The place where Paul Gauguin became a primitive, living with fourteen year old girls presented to him by their parents, and producing a large number of paintings in his unique style showing a proud, strong and carefree people. Robert Louis Stevenson and Herman Melville had visited. Both told stories of cannibalism in the islands.

Further away north of the equator in Hawaii was where Captain Cook, after three circumnavigations around the globe, died a grisly death. He found the Polynesians interesting. His death was a sad tragedy.

Captain Cook born in Yorkshire was brave, intelligent, a gifted sailor, navigator and map maker but he made a fatal mistake and had bad luck. At the time when we make decisions we don't know or even foresee some of the possible outcomes.

After Cook left Hawaii the mast broke. He decided to turn back for repair. Once anchored again in the bay a small boat of theirs, one of several used to get to shore, was stolen by some Hawaiians. Captain Cook and some of his men went ashore to retrieve it. A fight broke out. Cook was hit with a large stone and stabbed with a knife which killed him. He was later boiled in a big pot. His men later obtained some of his remains which they buried at sea.

Chapter Four

The next day on Nuka Hiva a brawny Polynesian man aged about forty five, spoke to us at the edge of the bay were I was washing towels at the quay. Water came from a clay pipe on to a large flat stone on which I had to pound, squeeze and pummel the towels used by Francis and Murray on their non-stop twenty six day voyage from California . There was no laundrette in the village. Nor was there a basin at the tap, there was just the rough stone. The towels and clothes felt heavy full of water. My fingers felt small in the large sodden fabric and felt too soft against the solid, grainy stone.

The man asked what we had to trade. He wanted .22 rifle bullets. We were taken aback at this first encounter in this tranquil place. Francis said we didn't have any. We didn't have a gun. I wasn't keen to trade anything. I didn't trust him. Francis, however, wanted to appear friendly so he agreed to trade a new tee shirt and a baseball cap for fruit and fish. We rowed back to Plainsong and got the items. I stayed on board. Francis went ashore and handed over the items. The man announced that he didn't have the fruit or fish with him but he would turn up there at nine o'clock the following morning to complete the bargain. I was annoyed with Francis for agreeing to give the cap with no two way simultaneous exchange.

The next morning Francis was at the agreed place ten minutes early and waited half an hour. Nobody turned up. He went back again at five o'clock in the late afternoon believing that the man had simply been delayed for some reason. He didn't show up. The old rule of commerce still applies wherever you are: caveat emptor – let the buyer beware.

The heat is stultifying. It is 90 degrees Fahrenheit by ten in the morning. Each day between noon and three I sleep or rest unable to cook or clean or even to stand. It feels way too hot especially with almost equal humidity. I feel like a dried out sponge. It feels as if all the moisture in my body has been drawn out in perspiration; as if the heat has sucked out every drop of water leaving me limp and depleted. At night time the temperature cools down to a hardly less comfortable 84 degrees. There are almost equal hours of daylight and night.

It is hard to believe that the missionaries made the Polynesian women wear dresses with collars and sleeves in this heat where even a swimsuit feels too hot. The rectangular pieces of cloth worn by locals, often blue with white flowers, are a perfect cover up, light and simple. It is what I wear now unless in a swimsuit.

Considering that there is no lagoon to protect Taiohae Bay we were lucky with the weather. It stayed calm while we were there. When Francis and Murray had sailed from San Diego the voyage took them twenty six days. After fourteen days out from San Diego the makeshift freezer, which was supposed to be kept going by running the engine for a few hours a day, stopped working. This meant that all those lovely succulent cuts of meat and other food, divided into daytime packs of two pieces that were intended to last for two months of a three month journey, that we had ordered a month before our California departure and picked up the day before leaving, had all gone off. Murray and Francis had enjoyed some but unfortunately I didn't get any. We had to throw away the fish, poultry and meat. The delicious fruit here made up for it.

One of the two fresh water tanks in the boat had become contaminated only one week out on their ocean journey. The water from it was pale brown with black bits in it. It needed to be emptied and cleaned out then filled with fresh drinking water. Meanwhile, we harvested rain water from short, sharp, heavy downpours. Resourceful Francis had rigged up a pipe for such an occasion leading from the centre of the bimini canvas cockpit cover which fed into a bucket on the deck. When it rained the bimini sagged in the middle allowing the rainwater to pour down the pipe into the bucket giving us fresh water. We tested our desalination machine which, after some considerable time pumping sea water, gave us two pints of clean drinkable water.

There was no fresh drinking water supply at Taiohae. The water at the quay was not drinkable. The only drinkable supply was at a bay known as Daniel's to sailors and Hakatea to locals. We headed there a few days later after enjoying eating and stocking up on small, aromatic bananas, thick skinned grapefruit (Pamplemousse) and papaya. Daniel's Bay is spectacular and smaller than Taiohae. It lies in a gentle bowl inside huge, vertical mountains. At the head of the bay is a beach and behind that several buildings which make up Daniel's house. Whispy smoke rises from two small fires near the house. Behind that and to the left is a tropical garden of Tahitian gardenia flowers, frangipane, banana trees, coconut palms, and breadfruit trees. The breadfruit has lovely shiny dark leaves and the fruit looks like a piece of corn sticking up from the branch. It must be cooked before it is eaten and is rather tasteless.

The coconut leaves are quite different from the banana. A coconut leaf curves towards the pointed end and each long leaf is made up of many small leaves. It has hundreds of long thin leaves looking like a fan wafting in the morning breeze. The coconuts hang in orange clusters high in the tree.

There are abundant banana trees, their bunches in five or six rows with as many as eight in a row. The bunches are long and wide and stand up. Polynesians say their bananas do not droop they stand up. It has a peeling bark and the leaves are six foot long with flat sides like the straight hem of a grass skirt, and not curved like those of the coconut tree. I had never tasted such delicious bananas. Of course, they are fresh straight off the tree; no shipping or pesticides. The South Pacific banana stems from the Cavendish family, Chatsworth Estate in England. The head gardener, Joseph Paxton, cultivated them from a gift given to the 6th Duke of Devonshire. These were sent with missionaries to various places including the South Pacific.

Bananas are my kind of herb. Although we refer to them as a fruit they have no seeds. I rather like the fact that they like freedom to go where they like; they do not like to be forced into rows. Their suckers find a patch of ground they like and dig in; They do not like to grow alone; They do best in clumps where they can shade each other's fruit from the sun with their large leaves; They rebel against intensive cultivation and pesticides. Has the Cavendish banana been pushed too far? Panama disease is wiping out the Cavendish all around the world. It is said that within a few years it will no longer exist. What are we doing to this beautiful fruit and herb? Are growers willing to treat the banana well and not intensively cultivate them?

Not all the fruit grown in Polynesia is native to the South Pacific. The banana is thought to have originated in Asia from India to Papua New Guinea. Some say Polynesians brought coconut, banana, taro and hibiscus to the rest of the world. In the late seventeen hundreds pineapple and guava were introduced from Brazil. Then tamarind, lime and mango arrived. In the late eighteen hundreds bougainvillea, hibiscus, and cacao which grow in warm sub-tropical and tropical regions were brought by an Englishman called Johnson. Frangipane and Lantana were brought in by Abadie and Chappe, two Frenchmen; Pamplemousse, the large grapefruit with thick skin, was brought from South East Asia by a North American, Harrison Smith. One of the most common and fragrant flowers is the Tahitian Gardenia, Gardenia Taitensis which is also known as Tiare Tahiti. Native to Polynesia this evergreen shrub has dark glossy leaves. It is a strongly fragrant, sweet, creamy white flower that is often worn in the hair.

Sitting with Daniel, after whom the bay is named, and his wife, Antoinette, I looked around their garden. We sat on a long wooden bench in an open kitchen. There was a small fire in the garden near the kitchen. The breeze blew the smoke along the garden keeping away the mosquitos and no-no flies. Saws, metal files and carpentry instruments hung on one side of a wall and kitchen equipment on the other. Their bedroom is in a walled part of the tin roofed hut. Their sitting room is the garden though there is a smaller one next to the kitchen which is open sided on three sides, the fourth side abutting the bedroom. There is a corrugated tin roof over the living area with palm leaf covering. There are no other buildings or people living in that bay. Antoinette and Daniel speak fluent Polynesian and French and a few words of English. Antoinette hurt her wrist two months ago yet her hand was still swollen. She had Ibuprofen. We gave her some aspirin and some cream to reduce the pain and swelling. Daniel has a hose to deliver clean, drinkable water from a spring and he rations it so that only one or two boats a day may take some. He told us we must wait until half six in the morning on the following day to fill the canisters for the water tank on our boat.

After filling our water canisters Daniel showed us his marvellous large albums and books full of notes and the signatures, photographs and drawings done by the sailors on all the various boats that had come into his anchorage and shared his water. He asked that we write in our boat too and where we had sailed from. The books start in 1988 and he was on to his third book.

Just before we left he and his wife presented us with a large package containing a dish with a feast of roast goat with onions, coconut milk, bananas and rice. The goat had been baked, Polynesian fashion, in a hole in the ground. Stones are used to keep in the heat once the fire is burning in the oven and leaves and sticks are used to cover the animal. The idea of it alarmed me but it tasted delicious. Here wild goats wander all over the mountain sides and it is considered the best meat. Daniel and his nephew had hunted and killed the goat. They leave it to cook all day in a pit. After living for days on soft cheese and tinned sardines the roasted goat tasted very good indeed.

I wouldn't like to eat goat every day because that would be pure greed to keep killing so that you could eat meat every day. It might be more acceptable to kill several animals a month when there is no other fresh high protein food. In fact here that is exactly what they do. Here animals are not intensively farmed nor injected with growth hormones.

This leads to another set of thoughts. When we approach an empty cove or bay I reflect that until relatively recently the people here were cannibals. I can tell you, it feels horrible imagining being prey!

Sunday 15th June. Leaving Daniels's Bay at eight in the morning we had a view of an unusual skyline: a small island in the distance with many high pinnacles of rock, thin like Bavarian castle turrets, as if reaching to pierce the sky.

The three groups of islands we were to sail in within French Polynesia are The Marquesas: hard rock high mountains, thick with lush vegetation of ferns, palms, bread fruit trees, and fruit trees such as mango and pamplemousse. Exotic flowers grow in the damp heat. There are no lagoons so the sea rushes in to crash against the land.

The Tuamontus are an archipelago of low-lying coral reefs just a few feet above sea level. They are formed from ancient volcanoes that have collapsed aeons ago leaving the rim to form the perimeter of a lagoon. There is no central island.

The Tahitian Islands, also known as the Society Islands, are an exquisite combination of both the landscape of the Marquesas with their soaring mountains and the Tuamotus with their protective, encircling reefs and shallow lagoons looking as if painted from an artist's palette of blues.

We motored away from Nuka Hiva for an hour in very light air. Having the engine on for an hour or two tops up the batteries which the solar panels do not do so efficiently. Sailed for six hours on a broad reach in pleasant winds. An uncomfortable swell only lasted for half an hour.

The island of spires ahead is Ua Pou. There is a tiny strip of land on a slope ending in the sea. The guidebook told me this was the airport. It can take no more than a twenty seater plane and that is infrequent. When you check in both you and your luggage have to get on the scales so that the plane stays within its weight capacity.

There are no roads around the island though some exist for short distances within villages and there are some tracks between them. Transport is by foot, horse or small motor boat. We headed towards the main anchorage of Hakahetau but seventeen sailboats were already there and those on the outer edges were rolling at anchor. The bay wasn't well protected so we went on to Vaiehu Bay. The weather turned squally, winds 15 to 17 knots with a choppy sea. We could see that Vaiehu was open to the west and although the wind was south it seemed to roll right in. We sailed on for Hakaotu Cove which turned out to be much better protected. It felt similar to the small coves on Santa Cruz Island in the Channel Islands of Southern California.

Four men are sleeping on the beach under a rock outcrop. They have a dog and two horses and are drying copra, coconut, which is a reliable and steady crop to sell on the commercial market.

Francis was full of beans and straining for adventure and exercise. He wants to walk to a village he has seen marked on a chart. It looks as if it is through jungle without a path. Tearing through the undergrowth does not appeal to me so I decide to stay onboard and read a book. Francis rows to the beach on high waves. The men drying coconuts help him ashore as he crashes through the surf on the dinghy.

It takes him an hour and a half to beat his way to a village. Francis walks through jungle with small decorative tins of leaf tea to barter for bananas. He returns triumphant with a huge stick of small, firm, fragrant bananas. Meanwhile, on board I've cut up netting to make hatch covers to keep out the mosquitoes.

Chapter Five

17th June. Well, with a mixture of fright and excitement, we are off. Yikes!

We set sail for the weirdly wonderful Tuamotu Islands. It will take five days of non-stop sailing in an empty sea to reach the Tuamotus. There will be no shelter from bad weather.

We left at half eleven in the morning. This is my furthest offshore passage. Twelve years earlier I sailed with friends from Plymouth, England to Howth, Dublin, Ireland then on to Scotland and the Outer Hebrides. The England to Dublin journey took three days including two nights of sailing. Oxnard, California to San Diego the previous month in May took the same time but we sailed along the coast.

Ua Pou looked lovely as we left, with its magnificent spires and mounds in the sunlight against the pale blue sky.

We have organized a system of watches. We will be flexible during the day about watches. At night we do three hour watches each starting at nine each night. The sun set at half five and I would do the watch until six and then nine o'clock until midnight. At nine at night two dolphins came and swam next to our boat for a while. The winds are light so we are sailing slowly and gently.

18th June I did my watches including a three to six am shift. The moon had gone when I came to do my watch. There was a sailboat in the distance on our port side all night which finally disappeared at five o'clock. I was sorry to see it go because its masthead light had been a reassuring companion through a dark, empty sea. It sat for a while like a small star on the horizon. Another boat on our starboard side but a couple of miles behind appeared at four o'clock. The sky was so black that it looked strewn with thousands of tiny diamonds and an occasional ruby.

For safety, Francis insisted that we cannot listen to the radio on watch nor can we use a light for reading because it would ruin our night vision. I have a writing pad on which I draw any patterns I see between the stars. In the daytime I will look up on sky charts to see if anything resembles what I have drawn.

During the day Francis and I discuss where we should stop in the Tuamotus. They are really a group of atolls: coral reefs around a lagoon.

Some passes into the lagoons have between seven and nine knots of sea. Our boat's speed on a good day is not much over five knots so I don't think we want to battle those currents. Others have difficult entrances and all have a lot of coral nearby, in the entrances and inside. We decide to skirt above the atolls and not anchor.

There was a squall in the afternoon which arrived just as Francis caught a tuna and was reeling it on board. The squall unleashed itself causing pandemonium on deck. I was at the helm steadying the lurching boat, spilling wind from the tight sails, rain pouring down drenching us while the wind was screeching around the mast. Francis got the fish on board where it jumped about thrashing its head and tail on the deck of the rocking, pitching boat. He hit the fish on the head with a winch handle and the fish became still. A bucket was ready in the cockpit where Francis immediately gutted the fish in the teeming rain. I couldn't have done it. I felt so sorry for the poor creature. If I was alone in the wild and had to kill things it is possible I would become very, very skinny – and hungry. We ate it later for supper with rice and onions.

We search the radio bands for the frequencies mentioned in the cruising guides. We are looking for a local offshore sailing net. This is a network or frequency that sailors use to call each other and broadcast information. We hear boats ahead of us sailing in the same direction talking about bad weather. There are gales ahead.

It is useful to have these marines nets because it is difficult and often impossible to pick up weather information so far from land. We tuned into a good marine net of sailors and hear that the Tuamotus are having bad weather and twenty five to thirty five knots of wind with a very rough sea. A boat called Dragon Air says it usually sails at five knots but is being blown at seven knots and sent skidding down high waves. It reports that at times the wind is changeable and coming from all over the place like a madman's footprints. A few boats are finding that the increased sailing speed means they will arrive at midnight instead of an arrival at dawn when they would have been better able to pick their way through the coral reefs. Now they will by-pass the Tuamotus and continue to Tahiti because it will be too dangerous to enter coral areas at night and at high speed.

It is half eleven at night and I am doing the ten o'clock to midnight watch. Francis and I have changed my watch from a three hour to a two hour shift pattern at night because I am finding it so difficult to keep concentrating as a look out for three hours alone on deck. Francis will do more hours at night and I will do more during the daytime. Two birds fly over the boat. One stays and is hovering my side of the main sail high above the spreaders. It stays, quietly drifting on an air current, for an hour. The sky is too dark to tell which type of bird it is even though there is a full moon. There are no boats in sight and it is pleasing to have the bird as company.

Between four o'clock and six am there is more wind. The sea swell is growing. The boat moves well through the water. The moon hides behind cloud for many minutes at a time. When it escapes to show its light it is a wonderful luminous gold. When it later disappears it lit up the shadow of a cloud the shape of a large mushroom. It is an ominous vision and a reminder of what happened in these waters for decades. The French, between 1966 and 1996, set off 193 nuclear explosions in the southern Tuamotus. Once the Polynesians realized the damage and destruction being caused they protested but to no avail until much later.

The night watches are causing a disturbed sleep pattern. In the short period between one watch and another I am lucky if I get an hour of sleep so in a whole night I might achieve three hours of sleep. Often I barely sleep a wink and try to catch up during the day. Tonight when I slept between midnight and four the sea must have developed into long swells. I dreamt I was riding on the back of a large elephant just behind its big, waving ears. I was holding on to its small fringe. The elephant was friendly and we zig-zagged through the windy sky, his ears flapping.

Ten am. There are large seas. The wind is between 15 and 18 knots yet the swell is high and long. This is not lovely viewing. We batten down the hatches. The wind picks up to 21 knots. We sail under reefed main and a storm jib. I repeat to myself the Reinhold Neibuhr saying :

"God, grant me the serenity to accept the things I cannot change, the courage to change the things I can, and the wisdom to know the difference."

There is nothing I can do about the swell. Nor can I go ashore. If things go well this swell will get no bigger and we will not hit bad weather. However, there is a long band of bad weather west and south of us and that is the direction we are heading. We set the windvane to steer and it does well. The wind increases with noise of its howling and screeching lashing against the sails.

Friday, 20th June. A terrible night. High winds with steep waves.

The weather worsened. That mushroom cloud did foretell bad weather, I think, as I check everything in the galley is secure. Plainsong is sailing without either of us at the helm because we are using the excellent Monitor Windvane. It has become so useful especially in bad weather though we still keep a lookout. We sailed in a grey fog sky all night from six in the evening until six in the morning. The clouds reached down to the sea, a dark blanket encircling us. Squalls hit several times an hour with winds between twenty five and thirty five knots. We are only half way to Tahiti. An awful thought. Neither of us got more than twenty minutes of sleep the previous day or night and by this morning we felt pretty awful until we saw a tiny blue patch of sky and hoped it would stay with us and grow.

The power of the sea throwing the boat around is not thrilling. At least not to most people. There are some sailors, Francis being one, who cross all sorts of seas knowing this sort of weather is likely to hit them and to them it is all part of the adventure. They like the adrenalin hit, the challenge to have the forces of nature and their own skill push up against each other as in a game, to come through it successfully. Francis enjoys the thrill of it all. He has sailed with a friend across the Atlantic and across the Northern Pacific from Los Angeles to Hawaii.

Off watch I lie on my stomach on a bunk and wonder if people who like fairground big dippers and fast, heart stopping rides would enjoy being on a boat in this weather. I lie groaning as every hard wave slams into the side of the boat making it shudder. I've never been sea sick but who knows what will happen next? We are simply two people bobbing around in a little boat in a storm making its way through the biggest ocean on earth. It is too noisy, too jarring, too turbulent to get any sleep or even rest.

Saturday, 21st June. Squalls all through the night.

For nearly two days we got no more than half an hour of sleep. My body ached with sleep deprivation and exhaustion. Just to stand upright, to keep a lookout when on watch braced against the cockpit and tied on by a safety harness to the rails was tiring. Just to do something simple like go to the loo was time consuming because it meant taking off my wet oilskins and boots in the cabin near the companionway so that water from them wasn't leaked throughout. This helped to keep the cabin and bedding dry.

Having a watch system doesn't necessarily mean you can sleep when off watch. Besides not being able to sleep in bad weather, sometimes in calm weather it needs two of us if there is a problem with the sails, to check the charts or something else needing attention.

The noise was so loud for so long that I forgot what normal was. Then silence by dawn. It feels strange and eerie after the howling, screeching wind for thirty six hours. No more clanking and crashing sounds of the saucepans and buckets, of the books and ballast as the boat was thrown down steep, steep waves in an empty ocean. The sheets of cloud that unravel down from the sky to the sea are empty of power. There is rain but no longer a buffeting wind.

I manage to get five hours of sleep during the day in two, two and a half hour batches. A luxury. It feels like bliss. The sea is calm, wind is a light seven to ten knots, the sky is blue overhead and to the south. There are showers I can see in the northwest. We are sailing with only the Yankee because we have decided to head for Ahe, an atoll about sixty miles away to the south west. That should allow a few restful days in the lagoon before going on to Tahiti.

The weather information gathered is that between Ahe and Tahiti it has been very rough for the past week and tomorrow the same. We have no desire or inclination to battle more wind right now. Two other boats we have spoken with on the marine net will have recently anchored in Ahe. They are Molucca III and Bonnie of Clyde.

All the sailors we have heard on the net sound very good. All are making long passages and some a circumnavigation of the globe. Molucca was always ahead of our course while Bonnie of Clyde was behind us until yesterday when she passed us though we didn't see either of them because they were too far away. We noticed the names of both boats when we were in Daniel's Bay but hadn't spoken to them there.

Francis is tanned from all the sailing. He is wiry and strong. He has good practical ability and no fear. We get along extremely well. He is a good companion and I am never bored. In sailing, as in so many sports, or jobs, and in life itself, you must have complete trust in those sailing with you, on a boat or the journey through life. Your life, here at sea, depends on them and they depend on you. They must sail well and safely; know how to contact other boats and send a mayday signal, how to stop a boat under sail if someone goes overboard, and essentially how to retrieve that person. It is particularly pleasant if you blend well together.

I did the evening 9 pm to midnight watch and then 4 am onwards. The sea was calm. It was a cloudy night so no stars were on show. At five o'clock it was a surprise to see a red light to starboard after all the darkness. It was another sailboat on its way, rapidly, to Ahe.

Woke Francis at half five, as agreed, so that we could check the charts and visually be on the lookout for the reefs of Ahe and the island of Manihi. These are not called "The Dangerous Isles" for nothing.

All the islands in the Tuamotu group, except we learned later, Makatea, are low-lying coral reefs. They are only a few feet above sea-level with generally single storey building and a few palm trees. The unpredictable currents and low coral reefs make this area a major navigational hazard. It is important to keep an eye on the chart, the compass course and a good lookout. Every year boats go aground on the coral and are lost.

Chapter Six

AHE 14 degrees 32 minutes south and 146 degrees 21 minutes west. It has only one pass. Ahe is only 14 miles by 7 miles and one of its discoverers was Wilkes, an Englishman in 1839.

Keeping a keen lookout we spied at six o'clock a grey, long smudge in the distance on our starboard side. This was the reef of Ahe. After working out high tide and slack water and enjoying a bright dawn it was decided to try and get through the Ahe reef pass in an hour's time instead of waiting another five hours. At noon the sun would be overhead and would provide better light to avoid the coral heads going into and once inside the lagoon. It is hard to see coral when there is shadow and when the sun is glistening on the water. However, the coincidence of our arrival so close to the pass entrance at slack water and the bright day encouraged us to make an earlier attempt.

The weakest current is generally one hour after low water and one hour after high water. For the previous four hours the current had been quite strong. This had made it hard to stay on our compass course and achieve the course we wanted. Knowing this we steered slightly above our course, steering 260 degrees and making the intended course of 250 degrees.

It took us a considerable time to identify the pass. The first place looked open at a distance but on closer inspection waves were breaking all along what had initially seemed to be a gap. A few miles further on there was a narrower break in the reef. Then Francis spotted a beacon marking the left side of the pass. We raised the mast steps to give a better, clearer view of any dangerous coral. The navigation book had said the course was central through the pass. Standing on the foredeck and looking ahead and then down it seemed there was coral all over the place even in the centre. It was dark brown in colour and it was simply impossible to guess the depth of the coral beneath the keel. Was it three feet below the water or ten feet, or twenty feet? The water was so clear that the coral looked so close. One false move and it would put a hole through the hull. The cruising book has made it sound as if we would sail over a clear sandy channel when it was actually a little sand strewn with jagged sharp coral.

Typical houses

It was a scary entrance not just because of the coral but because there were fast rip tides both to port and starboard only feet away. Thankfully the channel was well marked so Plainsong was steered down the centre still keeping a focus on avoiding coral. A large Copra schooner came in behind us catching up just before we reached the anchorage area. It was time for might to have priority and have right of way so our slow moving vessel pulled aside to allow the schooner to pass.

"Bonnie of Clyde" called us on the radio to welcome us and told us the ship had now anchored so it was safe to go on in. By 9 o'clock we had anchored. There were six other yachts anchored on this beautiful morning. I felt invigorated and full of beans. A couple of Americans from a nearby yacht came over in their dinghy, clambered aboard and explained that we could go aboard the schooner to buy food. A voice came over the VHF radio welcoming us. Michael and Susie aboard their boat "Chan" who also told us about the supply ship. It was a warm welcome from all the yachties in this far flung part of the globe.

The sandy roads on Ahe

Later that morning we rowed ashore in our dinghy. As I got to the prow of the dinghy ready to jump ashore I looked up to where I would have to leap. The quay wall was several feet above the dinghy. Just then a strong, young Polynesian woman yanked me up from the dinghy. It was so kind of her to give unasked for help.

We went onto a motor boat out to the ship for what we hoped might be a bag of fruit and vegetables and perhaps some biscuits as a treat. Well, I say motor boat, it was something that looked like a wooden four foot deep rowing boat in shape. It had no seats, just bare planks and a few tyres, a few huge gasoline drums and a large outboard engine clipped to the stern. There were five men clambering over and standing next to the oil drums smoking. The engines revved and we were off.

It transpired that the schooner was making its fortnightly visit to the islands to deliver supplies. It acts as a mobile shop and delivery service. The schooner anchored and small boats ferried goods and people ashore for the next two hours. People were taken from the shore in small open boats to the onboard shop which was a small metal fenced off area with a hatch where a thin, unsmiling man dealt with supply requests.

At the ship I had to hang on to a metal ladder slung over the side of the ship and jump from the bobbing wooden boat. At the top of the ladder I fling myself over on to the deck. I queued for half an hour to be served. There was no fruit or veg left. "Do you have fruit?" I had asked. "Non." "Do you have biscuits?" "Non." "Bread?" "Non." We left the ship which was more difficult climbing over from the deck onto the vertical ladder and at the bottom plopping on to the motor boat rocking up and down in the water. All the passengers this time were female aged from 15 to 30 and worked on the pearl farms.

Alice wearing local fabric wrap and a hibiscus flower

There was a big, strapping, attractive 40'ish woman about five foot nine in height driving the boat. She gunned the engines and we sped off at high speed, spray flying as we tried to keep our balance sitting on the old tyres. The driver cut a corner near a reef, zig-zagged in grand style then pulled up abruptly at the dockside, helped to slow down by banging into the outboard of an empty boat tied up ahead. Wow! These strong no nonsense Polynesian women are great.

Every afternoon low in the sky a narrow, scalloped band of white soft clouds sit above the horizon. There is not another cloud in sight. On the reef islets of white coral the rich emerald green of the coconut palms blow against the cerulean sky.

Mulloka III invited us aboard for drinks that evening, along with Bonnie of Clyde. We met Cliff, June and Neville, and Ian and Betty respectively after only knowing their voices on the radio. Good sailors generally don't drink alcohol while sailing. Now we were all anchored for a few days we could relax, have wine, or beer or whisky and chat the evening away exchanging stories. It felt like a band of brothers far from home living simple lives with just a few books and clothes some basic food and adventure in our hearts. Seven of us together under an unpolluted sky shining with stars, our boats bobbing gently at anchor while the wild sea rushed and stopped at the protecting reef.

There were no hotels or bars simply a small shop on this little atoll measuring 14 miles by 7 miles containing approximately one hundred and sixty people most of whom were involved in fishing or pearl farming.

The water at the shore was as clear as drinking water then it gradually became very pale blue, then turquoise, then dark blue at its deepest. Outside the reef the sea was the darkest blue of all. There were a series of motus that had formed around the lagoon and on these sprouted tall palm trees etched against the sky.

Monday 23rd June A clear sunny day with a light breeze. Had a quiet day catching up on sleep. Walked on the outer part of the atoll along a sandy path. One direction led to the rubbish dump. Nature is given the task of washing it away out to sea when there is a high tide. There are a few small shells but most of the atoll is chunks of bleached coral.

There is not an inch of grass or soil. Small plants struggle to survive, most do not. Some bougainvillea and hibiscus sprout here and there. Coconut trees provide the only shade, provide matting and roofing and are the most common edible crop. A single coconut can contain up to a litre of juice which has anti-bacterial qualities. The white centre or kernal once dried is the copra. The nuts are halved and left in the sun to dry for two days. The flesh is used in cooking. Once it is dry the kernal is removed and crushed to give coconut oil or milk. The crushed remains are not edible except by animals. Coconut is not a true nut but is a drupe. That is a fruit with a stoney covering of a seed such as an olive or peach. The fibre is used for coir matting while

Francis, Alice and local boy on Ahe

empty nuts provide bowls, or are burned to give charcoal and keep away mosquitoes. The trees provide nuts all year. It is safer not to sleep under the tree because one of the most common injuries and an occasional cause of death is being hit on the head by a falling coconut.

After our walk we went to the village to ask if anyone knew Norma and Ata and if they were here. I had met them and their daughter briefly just for an hour in Los Angeles. Both Norma and Ata spoke Polynesian and French and they were in Los Angeles to meet their daughter who they had sent to an American school. It was the end of term and they were about to fly home to Ahe with her. They had given me their names and addresses and asked that I contact them if I was in Ahe or Tahiti. It had seemed a remote possibility that we would be in Ahe because Francis had wanted to stop at other places. However, the other sailors and the weather favoured Ahe so here we were - to my delight. Now in Ahe I was told in the village that they lived at the other end of the lagoon and that I should ring them from the telephone office the next morning.

Woke at six to be at the telephone office by seven when it opened. It would remain open just for a short while depending on the number of people wanting to make calls. As we stood outside the office a couple came by and told us the office would not open until eight o'clock because most people, including the person who ran that office, were at a church service to celebrate the Saint of the church, St Joseph.

At eight o'clock a kind, handsome and western dressed young man told us that it would not open until nine o'clock. "Are you sure?" I asked. "Yes, yes. There goes the radio operator now," he said nodding towards two women passing us. Then as an aside he added "She's my sister." Feeling pretty hungry we decided to go back to Plainsong and have breakfast. We told the young man who we wanted to contact and he said their boat came this way once or twice a week.

Chapter Seven

An hour later and we were feeling content after a good breakfast of fruit and porridge. We were thinking of going to the dock again to make the call when a speedboat came by and knocked on our hull. We recognized the young man aboard as the one who knew Norma and Ata. He said their workers boat was in and he would tell them to come over to us.

Within two minutes there was a commotion outside our boat and Francis was on the deck jabbering away to the men in French. "Quick," he called down to me, "We have to leave with the men immediately." I put on my life jacket, grabbed my sunhat, sunglasses and two baseball caps to give as gifts and went on deck to see four strong looking Polynesians in a huge, quite basic wooden boat with no seats and outboard motor. It was Ata's workers on their way to the pearl farm. The brother of the radio operator had told them we wished to visit Ata.

We sat on a tyre resting on the floor of the boat and rushed along the rough water of the usually calm lagoon. Cool clear water sprayed us frequently from the breaking waves as the driver steered us between coral and the reefs to a self-contained community on a remote part of the atoll.

There were several pastel coloured single storey buildings belonging to Norma and Ata. Entering the house I was anticipating that they would not remember me, or worse – that Norma would not be on Ahe and Ata wouldn't have the foggiest idea who I was and would not like to be interrupted when busy working. Their eyes lit up when we met and they motioned for us to sit. Everything was fine.

Norma offered us lychees from a large bowl. As we chewed and sucked the fragrant fruit Francis spoke to them and translated for me their conversation. We all delighted in being inquisitive about the lives of each other. They looked pleased with the baseball caps we gave them as an offering of friendship.

In California when we met the conversation had been in English with their daughter and my tiny bit of rudimentary French vocabulary puzzling in my mind how to express my interest in them. I learned in Los Angeles that they lived some of the time on Ahe and some in Tahiti. They had chosen to send their daughter to school in the USA instead of to France.

Francis told them about our adventure, where we had set off from and where we were going. They showed us on a video recorder a group of men going fishing and catching a huge six foot Marlin. They invited us to share lunch with them and their workers at eleven o'clock.

Lunch was in what appeared to be a canteen. We left the small pastel square building with a corrugated metal roof and went a few yards in the sandy garden to another pastel oblong building of the same type.

To the right of the door was a long kitchen table, a chest high range of cabinets separated that seating area from the kitchen which was about eight feet square where we could see four women cooking and preparing lunch.

The other half of the room, in front of the table and kitchen contained two huge six foot tall stereo speakers and miscellaneous items against the wall. The centre of that room was clear. Large blackboards on the wall showed the location of all the oyster beds and the stage of development, and columns showing when last checked and when next to be checked and when they would be ready. Norma talked about pearls and explained to me how some pearls do not have grit manually inserted and are a pure pearl called keshi.

PEARLS: The black pearl is grown in Polynesia. It only comes from the Tahitian black lipped oyster "Pinctada Margaritifera". Several places farm it in the area including Rangiroa in the Tuamotus which caters well for tourists wanting to learn about pearls or to go diving. Rangiroa is the second largest atoll in the world with a coral reef sustaining a population of two thousand people.

Black pearls range in colour from pearly cream to grey through deep purple and black, which can have yellow or greeny blue tinges rather like those on a small oil slick. They are farmed mainly in the Tuamotus and the Gambiers.

Long ago one of the biggest businesses was harvesting oyster shells for mother of pearl to be made into buttons and exported. The invention of plastic buttons almost obliterated that market. Farming of oysters for pearls replaced that occupation.

If an oyster detects a small irritating bit of grit inside its shell it seals it off by coating it with a substance called nacre. In pearl farming this bit of grit or bead is placed in the oyster manually by specialists. Gradually the nucleus is covered with mother of pearl (nacre). If a nucleus is introduced by natural means without human interference such as a grain of sand or coral then it will produce a rare "fine" pearl.

Mother of pearl thickens at about 2 mm a year. Eighteen months later the harvest may be gathered. The Tahitian black pearls grow for between two and four years and are checked regularly to make sure the oysters are healthy.

Valuation of a pearl depends on several factors : lustre, iridescence, shape, diameter, quality and colour.

Keshi is pure mother of pearl with no nucleus usually measuring 2 to 8 mm. It is often baroque in shape (asymmetrical). Mabe is caused by direct human intervention by using a plastic mold stuck to the inner surface of a shell which is covered gradually with mother of pearl. After a few months the mother of pearl is cut off and the mold removed.

Our lunch was delicious Blue Marlin. The fish was sliced thin and dipped raw into either of the two cold sauces on the table. Other pieces were in chunks that had been marinated in lemon, salt and coconut milk then sprinkled with sliced cucumber and tomato. Wow! That was my favourite.

Then there were delicious hot small fish eight inches long and fleshy. They looked like plump trout. They were piled high on a serving plate with sweet brown fried onions. All this fish and huge bowls of rice were placed on a small table where Norma, Francis and I sat. We helped ourselves to the wonderful food before us. It was a feast fit for a king or queen. The fresh lemonade we drank with it was cool and tangy and so refreshing.

Big Ata, as I thought of him, sat at the main table several feet away facing towards us. Six of his workers, all men, joined him at the table. They talked and ate and drank soft, home made drinks. About forty minutes later the workers left and five more workers came in and sat for lunch with Big Ata.

Half a dozen women sat down for lunch in a different part of the room. One sensed hierarchy. Ata's presence filled the room. His presence was awesome. He was big and powerful and as a wide as a sequoia tree. He wore a thick, shiny gold necklace over his brown chest. I felt as if I was in the presence of the protype man that inhabited the earth. It was quite primitive this feeling. Unspoken yet communicated was a strong magnetic force and at the same time scary. He seemed to carry the genes of a long line of bright, brave Polynesians. Married to Norma, a beautiful, petite woman of five foot three with graceful movements who shared the business of the pearl farm and oversaw the meal preparation and cooking.

She and Big Ata had been born and brought up on the islands on Ahe and Manihi. Ata had moved to Papeete, Tahiti. After they married both decided they preferred their quiet Tuamotu life so they returned. Now they ran a successful pearl farming business. They would travel to Tahiti for shopping or business or when flying to California or to Japan for pearl meetings.

When we met in Los Angeles I had not asked nor been aware that they had this business. I didn't even know that pearls came from these remote islands. I was full of wonder when the men came to get us in Ahe to take us to Norma and Ata and told us they had a pearl farm. In their house they explained how the pearl is formed. Norma surprised me with a gift of several pearls known as keshi. It was a touching gesture and I felt humbled by their kindness.

After the men had finished, they and Ata went outside to attend to work. A boat with two workers was about to leave to carry out inspections of pearl sites so we would have to leave with them unless we wanted to go in the evening. We decided not to impinge on their wonderful hospitality and to go. We hopped aboard their boat carrying bags overflowing with of all sorts of goodies that Big Ata and Norma had insisted we take with us : pamplemousse, lemons, bananas, pineapples and about six pounds of fresh marlin.

I felt very happy to have spent some time with Norma

and Ata at their home where we saw and were a little part of their Polynesian life.

After our half hour boat journey back to Plainsong we were mentally and physically tired and fell into a deep sleep for an hour.

Later we shared our marlin with three other boats. The next day the young American couple who we met briefly in the Marquesas showed us what looked like two small freshwater pearls. They said they found both in one shell. The husband held them up near his wife's ears and said what lovely earrings they would make.

They both excitedly said how unexpected it was to find two identical white, thin, pearls in the same shell. I wished Francis hadn't told them earlier about our trip to my acquaintances at the pearl farm. It seemed that the couple viewed all of life as a competition.

Breakfast each morning includes thirst-quenching green skinned pamplemousse. Later in the day we eat mango. I slice down longways each side of a fresh mango. The exotic scent floats up. With a small knife I peel off the skin around the hard centre. Bringing the central part to my lips, I eat and suck the fruit as the fragrant juice spills around my mouth and fingers. Mango. It is like nothing else. Its heady fragrance fills the air and I close my eyes immersed in the scent and taste of my favourite fruit.

Chapter Eight

Maritime Radio Nets. We came across two organized nets for sailboats. One went from the North and Central America area for sailors going to the Marquesas while the second was from the Tuamotus on to the Tahitain Islands.

There were interesting boat names including Mulloka III, Bonnie of Clyde (from Scotland), Investigator, Tin Fish, Buddha's Thumb, Alfie and Panash. Then there were Doasa, Imega, Dragon Air and Kismet. The latter two doing weather reports for Fiji and Papeete.

In 2015 a couple from Canada sailing in the South Pacific put out an emergency call from their yacht when sailing in heavy seas 1,200 miles from land heading for the Marquesas. They had to abandon their boat and were rescued by a couple on another boat who heard the distress call on Pacific Net.

There are three excellent marine nets for the South Pacific, these are : Pacific Seafarer's Net which is sea and land based net and was involved in the rescue above, (www.pacseanet.com); Pacific Maritime Mobile Service Net; and Intercon. These three share a bandwidth (14300 kHz) and work well together. For long distance sailing information including safety see www.noonsite.com.

25th June. I enjoy spending some time looking into the sea wearing goggles to watch all the different yellow and blue small fish go by. Awful looking sea slugs make me grimace.

The next day the male of the American couple had visited the island nurse because his arm and hand were swollen and painful. He had, he thought, been punctured the previous day while swimming near a reef. He and his wife left Ahe that afternoon sailing to Rangiroa where there is a doctor.

27th June. Pull up anchor at 9 am and begin threading our way through the coral filled channel to the Pass. Cleared Pass at 10.40 am after a few minutes navigating a rough patch of tidal eddies. The forecast for next couple of days had been for calm weather.

Listened, as usual, for Dragon air's weather forecast just after 11 am. For the first time he couldn't get a readable signal from the French transmitting station. Because there was nothing to translate into English he and all of us then relied upon the 8 am weather forecast that had been delivered by Kismet or Domicile from Fiji.

All boats between the Tuamotus and Tahiti had calm and were motoring. Sailed some of the day in light 3 knot wind. Wind dropped further at night. Motored from 11 pm until 9.30 am the following day. Saw Rangiroa to starboard, a low, spiky reef.

28th June. Sailing gently along at three knots under a white sky of small ruffles.

Dapper Dan is a mile or so off on our port beam. The wind is cooler than it has been since I arrived in Polynesia. The Marquesas were extremely hot day and night; the Tuamotus almost as hot. The temperature now west of the Tuamotus seems more comfortable, at least it seemed so to a milky looking Brit. Wind 10 to 15 knots all day. Good sail close hauled.

5.50pm sighted Makatea Island, the last of the Tuamotus

on our heading. Suddenly a series of tall peaks fill the distant horizon and because of their shape and height Francis thinks it is Tahiti. This seems hard to believe because Tahiti is 130 miles away. We realize they are the hills of Makatea which we had forgotten was the only atoll not flat.

Sunday 29th June. Saw two shooting stars within ten seconds of each other just after 11 pm last night. Both came from the Corona Borealis one going left and one going right. Within a few minutes another one shot across from the opposite part of the sky. It's much busier than I realized up there in the distant sky.

It's hard learning stars from books because when you look into the sky I imagine I can see a particular constellation when it is in fact a mixture of two others. I've seen Venus rise where the sun has set and found the Southern Cross with its two leading stars to the east, Alpha and Beta Centauri. The Great Bear, also known as the Big Dipper, points up to bright Arcturus and I marvel at the giant Scorpio. The Coal Sack is very interesting sitting darkly in the Milky Way, yet near to it and so different is the millions of years old Jewel Box with its glittering colours.

30th June. Sailing fine all the next day until 7 pm when the calm sea started to get rough with the sea full of foam from high white horses as the wind increased to 18 knots. Plainsong is heeling and sailing fast with jib, reefed mainsail, and yankee flying. It is uncomfortable. It is odd to be going fast into the black invisible night with an increasing wind.

Paul of "Dapper Dan" called on VHF to say "Hi" and that he has put two reefs into the main. He thinks at this rate we may be at Papeete before dawn. I agree. I tell him that Francis is on deck putting in the second reef. It is almost 11 pm. The wind is a consistent 18 to 21 knots.

Waves are breaking over the bow. I forgot to close the hatch in the head and main cabin. A large wave sent several gallons of water over the loo, and also through the other hatch onto Francis's bunk. The chimney pipe for the cabin heater is rattling. I check it is secure. It is fine. There is nothing visible all around, except the white froth of the waves as they loom like buildings over us. Some waves hit us hard on the side of the hull making a loud, dull thud. Canisters and ropes move around and bash into their cupboards. All our cupboards and lockers have safety catches so that they cannot spring open and empty their contents when a hard wave hits. The noise of the contents and the lines, ropes, halyards, the screeching wind and crashing waves make it a deafening night.

It feels as if my innards are pulverized. My stomach feels like a busy washing machine. It is difficult to stay upright and keep balanced. Hard waves occasionally slam into the side of the boat, others end steeply dropping us down a wave with a sensation that my stomach is a few seconds behind my body in the descent. I lie on a bunk and pray for this bad weather to stop. It is hard not to be thrown onto the floor next to the bunk. I wedge myself in and try to think that before too long we will arrive at our destination. Mid-evening the sky lit up with multi-coloured explosions from the Papeete direction. What the hell was it? It turned out to be the beginning of Heiva, a three week festival of traditional culture each July.

Plainsong gets into the lee of Point Venus, Tahiti at one o'clock in the morning. Point Venus is where Captain James Cook in 1769 watched and documented the transit of Venus with Charles Green and Joseph Banks on behalf of the Royal Society in London to more accurately work out longitude. The distance from the earth to the sun worked out then, and that known now using radar only differs by an eighth of one per cent.

The wind subsides. Lights of Papeete, the sea port and

the airport are lit up on our port side. "Oh look, there's another boat," I say. "Where?" he asks. "That masthead light," I say pointing upwards. He bursts out laughing. "That's not a mast head light that's a plane coming into land. The airport's just nearby."

Until the 1960s Tahiti did not have a proper airport. Its population was about 37,000. When the French increased their presence for nuclear testing in the Tuamotus the population rose in Tahiti to 130,000.

There are so many lights in the town it was difficult to find our leading lights to show us the pass through the reef. We found it as we got closer. Francis with chart in hand guided our course through the marked channels with me at the helm slowly weaving our way in the darkness towards the light of the town. Anchored at quarter past three in the morning. Phew, are we tired! But not half as tired as when we arrived in Ahe. Our position is 17 degrees, 32 minutes south and 149 degrees 34 minutes west.

Waiting for the canoe race

Chapter Nine

14th July, Bastille Day. Today the French have a big celebration. What it means to the Polynesians I have no idea and wonder what they make of it. There is a military parade lasting an hour with several hundred troops in various smartly pressed uniforms. Some are on motor cycles driving slowly in lines, there is a fire engine and a few armored personnel carriers. The head honcho inspected the troops while a small military band provided what I supposed was intended to be the festive atmosphere.

To get to Papeete from Maeva we had taken le truck. It was a wooden framed bus with seats longways along either side. There are no handles and no cushions on the seats. They are a quick, efficient way to get around Papeete during the day where they rattle by every few minutes. Polynesian women and men fill the bus. The women seem more self assured and unselfconscious than any women anywhere. They sit wearing a pareo (sarong) or strappy tops and shorts and flipflops; their plump bodies with rolls of fat around their middle are admired by the men. It is wonderful to see women unconcerned about their weight.

One of the highlights of our stay and a real treat was to attend a traditional dance competition. It was necessary to book in advance so we got tickets a week before. Each group consisted of between fifty and one hundred and fifty dancers. The females often wore long, thick grass skirts and a grass necklace over what looked like small, polished halved coconuts covering their boobs. They shimmied and wiggled to the frantic drumbeat. Their colourful, spectacular costumes were made partly of palm leaves and bright flowers. Many of the male dancers had tattoos on their thighs or ankles and often on their arms. Unlike much of Western dancing there is no thrusting of the body, simply the sensuous swaying of the hips.

Papeete is a busy, commercial town easy to walk around. There are good bakeries and cafes so Tahiti is a paradise of Polynesian life with delicious French food!

There is a regular canoe race each year with participants from many of the islands. Men and women stand at the shoreline in Papeete wearing garlands on their head waiting for their turn to race with their teams. The atmosphere is festive, happy and with a serious competitive edge. Surfing and canoeing are an imprtant part of polynesian life. Canoes are still used by some to commute to various places.

Two days later we visit The Gauguin Museum. It is about 40 miles away from Papeete on the coast. It is small and modern with many prints but few original paintings. It has an excellent series of photographs with interesting in-

Tahitian women by Gauguin

formation about his life. His art is often considered primitive which he may have aimed it to be. They give a realistic impression of the environment in Polynesia and the physique of the people. He admired their strong, heavy frames yet he does not convey any emotion in the countenance of the people.

In his private life Gauguin corresponded with his wife who he had married in his twenties. He left his office job in Paris as a stockbroker to paint, against the wishes of his wife and more conventional friends. Then he left his wife and five children. He earned hardly any money from painting and moved around to Deauville, Arles and Martinque always painting, never staying long. He was friends with Van Gogh and Degas with whom he discussed style and colour.

Getting a passage to Tahiti he explored French Polynesia and by 1891 he was living in Tahiti where he spent most of the rest of his life. He did make the journey several times back to Paris where his paintings were successfully being sold but did not earn him much money. By 1901 he was settled in Hiva Oa, an island near Nuka Hiva, in the Marquesas, where he spent the last two years of his life. He had a series of live in young mistresses and many sexual liasions. Mothers would offer their teenage daughters to him for sex. To Polynesians sex was fun and part of being hospitable. There were not many things that were taboo. Taboo and tattoo were originally Polynesian words.

It seemed odd that an intelligent middle aged man, western educated who had lived in Peru and Paris and in whose culture it was taboo to have a relationship with such a young woman should throw all his Western rules away and throw himself completely and utterly into a endless frenzy of sex. Then again, coming back to the books about sex and humans perhaps this is simply the male of the species doing what he most wants to do with no boundaries. In the middle ages in Britain and Europe many young girls were married between the ages of twelve and fifteen.

He intended being remembered as a great artist using a primitive style and he intended to have sex when he liked. The personality of the female was irrelevant. Like so many selfish or immature men he equated the silence or sullenness of females as a sign of mystery. The less they said probably the better. He could then imagine their wisdom and intelligence whether or not they had any. Therefore they could not interfere with his sex life or his work.

"He drew like a child and was just a dirty old man," one of the visiting sailors said to me. Yet, for all that, he was one of the few Europeans who painted people of other ethnic groups exactly as they were, in their true light with the real tones and natural posture. He did not change the shape of their eyes, the nose or their physique as almost all other painters did. He gave us a clear picture of some of the people of those islands. He made them proud to see themselves bold and true.

He travelled between Paris and Polynesia many times. He suffered from syphilis and died of an apparent heart attack on 8th May, 1903 in Atuona on Hiva Oa, the Marquesas.

Gauguin wrote to a friend that writers and artists communicate with the imagination, that they communicate with some part of feelings rarely touched except by genius. Maybe he is right and that it is a rare person who by their work can move others deeply.

While on Tahiti we enjoyed a land tour of the island in a rented car visiting Venus Point and the Museum of the Isles, a fern grotto and a botanical garden. The botanical garden was started by a young American, Harrison Smith. He had been a professor at the Massachuetts Institute of Technology in Boston. He moved to Tahiti where he remained establishing a large collection of plants amounting to about 450 species.

24th July. Off to the island of Moorea, opposite Tahiti. Under way by 10 am. Earlier in the still morning air whisps of curling smoke rose from various parts of the lower hillside as families lit their dawn fires. Motored to Papeete from Maeva. We went to and fro several times to check our compass alignments. We have three compasses in use. One is in front of the helm so good for the helmsperson. The second is in the cockpit near the companionway and visible to the helmsperson. However, this one is set and adjusted for the Southern Hemisphere so that when Plainsong gets close to Cape Horn where compasses often jam, this one will have no problems. The third is inside the cabin next to the chart table at the instrument panel and is offset by 90 degrees. This is rather clever because it allows it to be read by the person sitting in the companionway in bad weather keeping a lookout and keeping sheltered, as well as using it any other time.

Island of Moorea

Good sail to Moorea (yellow lizard) with 16 to 18 knots of wind. Big swell about 6 foot for an hour in the middle of the channel between the islands. A bit blowy closer to Moorea for our approach.

Many boats were anchored inside the reef rather than further into the main part of the Bay. We went in almost to the head of what is called Cook's Bay. Captain Cook visited Moorea anchoring in the nearby Opunohu Bay.

Mountains raise dramatically from the sea with a narrow section only a few dozen feet wide around the edge where the island road runs. There are several passes through the reef including passes into the two large bays and at Vaiare where the Tahiti ferry docks.

That night I was woken by one of the sounds I most dislike: that of a dog howling, frightened, hurt accompanied by aggressive barking and growling of other dogs. Dogs here are often in packs. Even when there are only two, one will usually attack the other until it lies belly up, paws folded. The dominant one then straddles it a while, occasionally growling so that the weaker one cannot move, or it stands nearby menacingly. Reminds me of gangs of male humans who pick on someone, usually a male, who is alone and perhaps does not look like them, and beat them up. So much for our supposedly advanced human species.

Explored Moorea. Drove up to Belvedere lookout where there was a fantastic view of both Cook's Bay and Opunohu Bay sparkling blue on either side of a rich, luxuriant hillside. Much of the hill is cultivated with pineapples, papaya and vanilla. There are fertile fields with goats and cattle. Enjoyed papaya tart at Stephanie's Café. We were told the owner, Stephanie came from Manchester in England. Sadly she wasn't there the day we enjoyed her cake.

The entrance sailing into Cook's Bay is well marked with large green buoys and red buoys guiding boats through the reef. We anchored in 55 feet of water near the head of the bay.

Francis cleaned the hull somewhat where vivid green tentacles had been successfully growing. Afterwards on the shore I cut his hair, which had also successfully been growing. He was rather anxious that my work would be a disaster. I didn't know why he would worry. We were in the middle of nowhere and friends back home wouldn't see it. It was fine and he enjoyed the feeling of clean hair and the breeze on his neck. There was hot water on the boat because we had run the engine. Washing my hair in hot water felt wonderful and surprisingly soft after so many weeks using cold water.

Later, in the darkness, we heard men singing natural and spontaneous near the shore. The South Pacific makes me open-mouthed with its beauty and isolation.

At night the constellation Scorpio is above the mast while the Southern Cross stands over the head of the bay. Venus is over the mountains to the west and the Corona Borealis to the north east. How beautiful the heavens are; a dark, rich blue canopy sprinkled with thousands of sparkling jewels.

The following day we visited part of the lagoon where

bottle nosed and rough toothed dolphins are kept in captivity and people may swim and pet them at set times of the day. Most of the dolphins are retired from work for the navy and cannot go back to the wild because they are used to people and ships. Some of the dolphins have been nursed back to health after injury and they too would not be able to survive in the wild. Dolphins that can survive in the wild are set free because it would be cruel to imprison them. In the water with them they feel smooth yet firm to the touch. They were five foot long, pale grey with long noses and very gentle.

Alice in lagoon with dolphin

29th July. Pulled up anchor at half seven on a still, clear morning and motored out of the bay towards Tahiti. Spotted eight whales swimming towards us. They were blowing water vapour which looks like steam 8 feet into the air about a mile away. These are the first whales I've seen since California. These were unusual ones I hadn't seen before. The shape of the head was more square than Humpbacks or Minkes. They were longer than our boat by around 10 feet with not much of a dorsal fin more like a lump. They looked like Sperm Whales which grow to 60 feet and can submerge for 70 minutes at a time.

30th July. Back in Tahiti I went to an internet shop and retrieved phone and email messages, the first time for two months! Later Francis presented me with an early birthday present – one of the black Tahitian pearls given to me by Norma and Ata has been set in gold to form a pendant hanging on a fine gold chain. It is a thoughtful present and I wore it immediately. Back at the pontoon the wind was blowing strongly again making it difficult to stand. Wearing my red life jacket I stepped into our small rubber dinghy then a propane gas container was secured in the bow tying it to the bright yellow seat. We were a few hundred feet from the shore so had not brought the outboard motor. Francis rowed back in bumpy conditions and we didn't get very wet. The wind was 25 knots, a normal amount of wind in the South Pacific, so that even in the lagoon there were little waves. Before sailing here I had erroneously thought that the wind strength would be similar to southern California where it is generally light at 8 to 12 knots. Out in the Pacific it is usually 25 knots. I put the kettle on and put away my necklace in a safe place until I was leaving the boat for England.

Plainsong is being got ready for the next leg of her journey to Pitcairn Island, then Easter Island then Chile. I'm not doing that part of the voyage. A diver had been arranged to visit to scrub Plainsong's keel so that it is smooth and will cut through the sea better without the small barnacles and the grass skirt she is currently wearing.

The diver did not arrive yesterday or the next morning. Dave, the sailor from Manana, offered to dive down and do it later that day. He is a great guy. He and his lovely wife, Marcia, and their cat, Motor, have spent the last twelve years sailing about the world. We took Plainsong to the fuel dock a mile away, filled her up and also replenished the water tanks.

Back at anchor Dave came aboard for a cup of tea and maybe to dive and clean the boat. Just as I passed him a mug of tea the diver arrived.

In the evening another sailor, Thierry, came over with his Tahitian girlfriend to have a glass of wine. He had been a cook on board submarines working for the French Navy. Thierry retired four years ago aged just 32! Sitting in the cockpit we heard the deep, soft sound of men singing joined by the Hawaiian ukulele. We could just make them out in the darkness as they sat under mango trees. We opened our one bottle of Champagne which had been given to us as a present when we left California. It was a celebration of the end of our two month South Pacific cruise because I would be a land lubber again in a couple of days. It had been a fabulous experience.

3rd August. Marvellous clear day in Maeva, near Papeete in Tahiti. Both the mountains of Moorea and of Tahiti are in full view with not even a tiny circle of cloud around the peaks. This is the first time in a month that it has been so clear. Plainsong and the half dozen other yachts gently rock on their moorings. We rowed in the dinghy to a shallow part of the lagoon to look at fish around the coral heads. It was amazing. Neither of us had seen such clean water as clear as drinking water. The sea plants, the urchins and fish were visible without putting my head under water and wearing goggles. Some of the plants resemble giant cabbages with four inch legs growing all over them, bobbly in formation waving slowly in the current.

Chapter Ten

6th August. Chris Chan arrived from Canada as Francis's crew to Chile. They got in contact via the Cruising World website. Went into Papeete to visit the Customs Office and Port Captain's Office to complete formalities to register Chris boarding a vessel in French Polynesia and me departing the vessel.

The next day we loaded the dinghy with my holdall and some bags of food. It's been a hell of a couple of days as I packed up some belongings in a turbulent lagoon trying to maintain my balance as I stuck my head into cupboards and lockers to retrieve passport, books, clothes and sandals. Leaving much behind for the cold sailing in Patagonia and Southern Brazil.

Francis gives me a hug and a kiss of au revoir. I had made breakfast on the boat for the three of us. Chris also finished off his noodles and peas from the night before. Chris and I go to Papara at the other end of the island where I will stay, I hope, for the next month. I wanted to get to know Tahiti better and to visit Bora Bora, which Francis wasn't interested in seeing. I have booked into a type of guest house. It does not always serve breakfast or any other meal. It is a place where each guest room is a separate thatched building set in the large garden. Each room simply has a bed, a couple of chairs, a low table, a tiny kitchen open plan only about 3 foot square and a small bathroom. It does have a small television showing a few French channels.

I bring the mosquito net with me from the boat. It hadn't been used. Chris and I fix it to a central light fitting above my bed in the guest house. I couldn't have done this alone because I couldn't reach. I've also brought some mosquito repellent coils and spray. I thank Chris and he departs for his adventure. At half eight that night Francis telephones the guest house and the owners come and get me. I make my way between the mango trees in the dark. He says the forecast is good so he and Chris will set off tomorrow. They will be heading in my direction so I might see them in the distance.

The next afternoon at two o'clock I saw a little white triangle in the distance. I grabbed my sunglasses and binoculars and went back to the garden to have a better look. Yes, it was them! They had two sails up not three because there was a strong wind. I watched as Plainsong moved fast and then changed course so that I could now see her stern. They sailed on towards the horizon and slowly disappeared heading for Pitcairn Island which would take an estimated twenty three days.

The owner of the guesthouse told me that it was difficult to get steady workers in the islands. They do not keep Western hours. Though he has had a gardener for fifteen years since the gardener was a teenager. On some days during the month the gardener will say to him "I'm not working for you for the next two days (or two weeks!) I fix my canoe," or because "I go fishin." The locals work to get what they need for the next month or so; they buy large sacks of rice and other staples and then stop work until they need to replenish supplies. This attitude I like very much. It doesn't suit a greedy capitalist economy but it sure suits life here.

Sunday, 10th August. A surprise phone call came this morning at ten o'clock. It was Thierry, from his boat 'Dominaut' also anchored in Maeva Beach wishing me a happy birthday. He suggested we go and look around the island. An hour later he was there smiling in his little old Renault. He kissed me on both cheeks and I introduced him to Madame Paris. They chatted away in French while she told him, laughing, that I had arrived there with a bag of lemons and grapefruit when there were plenty growing in their large garden that I was

Tahiti

welcome to eat them at any time. I had noticed the fruit but hadn't wanted to presume I could just help myself. Thierry and I said Au Revoir to Madame Paris and we set off. It felt wonderful to have some company. Thierry is handsome and a good conversationalist.

Thierry drove to the peninsular called Tahiti Iti, Little

Tahiti. On the way we stopped for a good lunch in a Chinese restaurant at Port Phaeton. This is a quiet, peaceful anchorage not a port in the sense of busy ships and docks. The restaurant looks out across the pretty bay. All through lunch one or other of us had to keep consulting my French dictionary when we were stuck on a word or expression.

Tahiti Iti is quite different from the main part of the island. It has few palm trees and looks like New England, USA or even Old England. Brown, healthy looking cows munched in lush flat-ish fields amidst gently rounded hillsides.

There is a magnificent viewpoint on Taravao plateau. It looks down over the isthmus which is at the very narrow waist of Tahiti and divides it from the less mountainous Tahiti Iti. I could see the island curve up from the isthmus to the left and then to the right. The reef, like a scalloped trim of whipped cream followed softly the shape of the island. Thierry gave me a hug as we looked out to sea then attempted to kiss me but I shook my head. 'I can try' he said smiling. I laughed and we walked and talked for an hour. He told me he might head down to New Caledonia and spend a couple of years there. We headed back to my place where he dropped me off.

Back in my room I'd been reading a book for a quarter of an hour when Dave of 'Manana' telephoned and sang 'Happy birthday' down the phone! Francis must have asked Thierry and Dave to make sure I wasn't alone on my birthday. So kind of him, and of them to agree. Dave had spoken to Francis that morning on single side band radio and all was well on Plainsong. We arranged that I would visit Manana on Tuesday morning for a coffee.

Monday, 11th. Mosquitoes exist here in their thousands. Every night I climb into bed surrounded by my extremely useful mosquito net. I have to do this at seven o'clock in the evening because the light in the room attracts them and they come in through tiny gaps between the walls and the ceiling roof. If it wasn't for the net I would be eaten alive. They buzz around all evening so I have to light an insect repellent coil. They look for gaps in the netting but there are none so I am safe. Unfortunately if I get out of it for one reason or another, to perhaps make tea, then the dratted little flying needles try to get inside the shelter so that they can bother me later in which case, if they do, a battle ensues until cursing and tired with twisted bedding I eventually kill the blasted creatures.

The floor in my room when I wake in the morning is covered with a couple of hundred dead mosquitoes. Thank goodness for the mosquito repellent coil. It does make breathing difficult but the alternative is worse.

It began raining early morning and didn't stop all day. There is one window with glass and another with no glass and a wooden shutter. If you close this then the room is almost completely dark because daylight cannot penetrate. Because of the heavy rain the window square was closed. I was burning another insect repellent coil but it made me dozy because there was no fresh air.

Mr Paris told me that he once owned a house next to the lagoon. Every few years there would be a bad storm and the house would be badly damaged. One night the wind was blowing at 60 knots, the roof blew off and the interior was damaged. He fixed the place up, sold it, and vowed never to own property on the sea shore again. Ever since then he has lived happily on this sheltered hillside, a mile from the lagoon.

He showed me a tall wooden platform about ten feet high and thirty feet from his house. It had white plastic legs dangling down and lying on top. "This is going to be a tourist attraction," he said pointing to the edifice. "I will show what the cannibals did." I was horrified. The white legs looked quite like the colour and shape of my own. It is not established that cannibals lived in the Tahitian Islands though they did live in the Marquesas and Hawaii.

On Tuesday I caught the half eight bus in the morning carrying a bag full of lemons and grapefruit for Dave. It took fifty minutes to get to Maeva beach, just before Papeete. Had a good morning and lunch with Dave and Marcia leaving them for the three o'clock bus back to my place. Dave had spoken by radio to Francis the day before and that morning. All was fine though they were becalmed that morning and had to motor.

By Wednesday I was fed up with the mosquitoes and the rain. When the rain stops I can't sit outside because I get bitten. I've decided to go into Papeete the following day and find alternative accommodation. There is more to do in the town especially when the weather is bad and there are more people around so it is interesting. It also means I can go to an internet café and pickup any messages there and to the Poste Reste run by American Express in the town. This allowed me to have an address where cards and letters can be sent to me.

Good post – three cute birthday cards from my family and a long letter from a friend. Got an email from Francis too telling me about the weather and how the equipment was faring.

While in Papeete I booked into the hotel for a night. Oh bliss! A clean, modern hotel with no insects. Enjoyed a good meal with green vegetables, the first veg I've had for some time. At dinner, stupidly, for the first time when travelling I asked for water to drink and didn't specify mineral. The waiter brought me a glass and jug of water and I thirstily drank three glasses of it. Later in my room I splashed about in a foamy bath. When getting dried I noticed a rash all across my stomach. I went to reception and asked if they knew what it was. I felt fine but my stomach didn't look it.

They said it was a reaction to the water and gave me bottled mineral water to drink with sugar stirred into it.

The rash was still there in the morning. It had spread to my arms and legs. I went to Claude who worked nearby at Tahiti Aquatique who does first aid to see if he had any ideas. "Water," he said. "you'll be fine. Just don't drink the tap water."

Waited at the bus stop for an hour and a half to go back to the guest house. Mr Paris had said the buses were every twenty minutes. A young man at a gas station across the road signaled to me that there were no buses that day. It was true. It turned out it was a public holiday. Mr Paris had neglected to tell me that. It was 20 miles to where I was staying. I looked for a phone box and found it only took cards not coins. The post office selling cards was closed and the shops that were open didn't sell them. A woman was leaving the phone box and I asked if she would let me use her card to ring a taxi and I would pay her. She said her husband was a taxi driver and would take me. Within fifteen minutes we had agreed the rather high fare and were on our way.

Later in the week I went to have lunch with Philippe and Jackie Pleutin. They are friends of a good friend of mine in England. The Pleutins are from Paris and teach physical education at the local school. They have taught in Tahiti for four years with another two years to run of their contract. We shared a delicious lunch starting with pate and bread followed by John dory fish in coconut milk with onions and tomatoes, followed by soft cheese and crackers. Drank two glasses of white French Chablis. Rather enjoyable especially as I've hardly drunk any wine in three months.

They have a beautiful and fragrant garden with jasmine, gardenia and bougainvillea. The sitting room has mementos from the various places they have travelled including wooden bowls and carving from New Guinea, the Marquesas, and

Chile. Philippe would like to move on at the end of the contract to another new place but Jackie has had enough of moving.

They offered to take me to the ferry at a quarter past six on Monday morning because I wanted to visit Bora Bora. They are a terrific couple and it was kind of them to offer to take me to the port.

Back at my place I was, as so often, staring out to sea. The sea was quite dark because of a small amount of cloud. The sea was just a little rough. All of a sudden about a mile or two off shore the water seemed disturbed. White foam frothed where it didn't normally. Looking through my binoculars it was hard to tell what was causing the boiling water. It was a mystery.

I'm reading John Gray's 'Isaiah Berlin' and am struck by the intelligence of Berlin and his ability to provoke thoughtfulness. Such people give talks in places of learning. What a gift it is when they give talks to the public not just to academics; giving talks to the general public in meeting halls and libraries so that anyone can have their intellect stimulated. Television and radio are excellent mediums for sharing ideas yet there is something special hearing a good speaker or a good and charismatic speaker in person in front of you. Bill Clinton, Grayson Perry and the marvellous French Minister of Foreign Affairs, Dominique de Villepin, who got unprecedented applause for his brilliant speech at the UN against going to war against Iraq, all have charisma and it is a treat to listen to them.

Mr Paris agreed to allow me to use his telephone to ring up Bora Bora to find a place to stay for a few nights. He hung around the room listening and I felt it was to see where I was staying and how much I was paying, I could see in his face he was wondering whether he should charge me more for my room. He has made me feel like a prisoner.

When Francis and I visited him to find out about accommodation Mr Paris was all helpfulness. "We will make sure you have a big fridge to keep your food fresh (no); we will take you to the shops anytime and will take you with us when we go (no); we will take you sometimes into Papeete (no); we will live like family (no). They didn't do any of it. I found them both distant and cold.

I think I understand how the character in "Typee" the Herman Melville novel about the Marquesas felt. He was kept a prisoner for a while by cannibals who were polite to him, fed him (to fatten him up) and wouldn't let him leave their tribal area. I long to leave and get excited when I have a day away from this place. This is a crazy way to exist so I will be moving out as soon as possible when I get back from Bora Bora.

The Pleutins kindly take me to the ferry. On the way they tell me of their concerns about the locals. Most weeks people are killed on the road by inexperienced drivers, by bad drivers or drunk drivers. They are also worried about the health of young people. Before high volume tourism and big hotels and importing foreign food and drink, the locals ate and drank local food and fruit. The local food was good for them, the Pleutins said, especially the coconut water which is anti-bacterial. "Now the young people eat too much food, too often and it contains too much sugar. Look at the high amount of sugar in soft manufactured drinks. They didn't need all this processed food," Philippe said. "Think of all the waste it produces, all the plastic bottles when once they ate the fruit and the fruit skins were burnt with burnable rubbish every so often."

"By the way, yesterday late afternoon" Philippe said, "a large pod of humpback whales were sighted swimming between Tahiti and Moorea." That was what I'd seen causing the disturbance in the water. Fantastic!

The ferry took four hours and 98 miles to reach the island of Huahine, just slightly south and east of Bora Bora. Reading the booklet on the ship it said
'In 3 years of operation they have sometimes encountered rough seas but our crew because of its professionalism knew until now how to handle the situations.'
'You will leave Tahaa with regrets.'
'Hills rise from 100 metres up to 300 metres, black stones everywhere strangely shaped cloning the god "Hiro's" part of anatomy'!
We stop briefly at the islands of Raiatea and Tahaa which share the same lagoon. Small dark green trees grow on top of white beaches on the small motus circling the lagoon. It is 5 o'clock when we reach Bora Bora in light rain. We travel some miles outside the reef to approach the one and only pass. Raiatea has 8 passes. The little hills are invisible because of the low rain clouds almost to the ground. Six sailboats were anchored nearby and soft sunlight peeped out and shone down on them. It was rainbow weather and indeed one appeared in just two minutes.
Caught an extremely full Le Truck to Chez Pauline's for the night. All holiday makers with back packs and soft luggage.
Chez Pauline's was quite an experience. Charming if you like to sleep in a windowless room. It was a house (fare) raised a foot off the ground with two Polynesian windows. The same type of windows as in the Marquesas and Tuamotus. It is a square hole in the wall. When it is daytime there is a wooden cover that is pushed out and held out with a three foot wooden pole. Of course, this means that at night time to stop mosquitos or men invading the room you

must remove the pole, the square wooden board then closes across the hole and there you are with four walls and not a bit of sky in sight.

The ceiling, made of pandanus leaves, rises to a point high in the centre. Apart from the double bed there is a small, narrow wardrobe and a shelf next to it. That's it.

At reception the helpful member of staff provided me with my requests: a blanket because there were only sheets on the bed; a towel because there were none; and matches for the mosquito coil.

Booked out at eight in the morning because I was woken at three o'clock at night by a couple of attacking, buzzing mosquitoes that wouldn't give up. I tried sleeping with a sheet over my head but the heat was stifling and there was no fan. I gave up trying to sleep. I put the light on and lit a poisonous coil and tried not to think about the coughing it was making me do. I read until 6 when I could open the window.

Tramped along the road with my beach bag in hand after breakfast looking for a decent place to stay. Walked in sweltering heat for half an hour before I found a proper hotel not simply a motel type place. When I asked for a room they asked 'Where is your husband?' and presumably because I was alone they said they had no rooms. After another half an hour walking in the heat I found another hotel and they too asked 'Where is your husband?' and although they had over 200 rooms, much like the previous hotel, they told me, I thought incorrectly, that they had no rooms available. Or rather I should say, none for a woman travelling alone.

Found a hotel truck to take me to my last and final attempt at a hotel. It was the only other one on the island. When I got to reception I had had enough of being told there were no rooms. The writers Paul Theroux and Bruce Chatwin travelled the world and nobody asked them where their wife or husband was. Nobody questioned their right to explore. Men were being treated better then women. Before saying anything, this time I snapped my American Express card down on the counter and then said I wanted a room for the night. They glanced at the card and then at me. They agreed but said it was a very expensive room. Fine, I said.

I nearly fainted when they took me to it. It was sooo gorgeous. It had a large sitting room, tastefully decorated, a large bedroom with a romantically draped four poster bed; a lovely bathroom, a small sitting room off the bedroom; outside the large glass doors to the private terrace stood a rattan table and chairs, delightful comfortable lounge beds and a wonderful private, small, pale blue swimming pool. It was a pool to dip into and float in rather than do lengths. It was lavish.

It was Hotel Bora Bora and one of the best hotels in the whole of Polynesia. It was an Aman hotel so I knew it was going to be incredible because I'd seen two other Aman hotels in Bali, Indonesia. It was a marvellous treat.

There were fresh flower arrangements on tables, on the bed, in the bathroom and fresh fruit sliced up and displayed on a plate in the main sitting room. All I had wanted was a clean room where I wouldn't be bitten by mosquitos.

However, I had to dash away ten minutes later to a small pier nearby because the lagoon snorkelling and picnic boat was about to depart. The Pleutins had suggested I do a boat tour because I would see so much.

A glass bottom boat took five couples and me out to different reefs within the lagoon. One was called the rose garden because of the floral shapes and colours. We stopped at three different sites for snorkeling. The driver, Tapee, who was a dive master asked why I stayed on the boat and didn't go into the water. I said it was too deep and I'd be afraid. I could see what I wanted to see from where I was.

He insisted I put on a buoyancy vest and wear goggles and I'd be fine. Once in the warm water it was lovely and I saw beautiful purple and deep blue coral and yellow and green coral. There were small and medium sized fish including lemon peel angel fish, emperor angel fish, convict tang and yellow Moorish idol.

Completely at ease at sea or in shallow water, strangely I don't feel comfortable in that in between depth where holes and rip tides, and sharks and rays are hidden.

Tapee swam like other Polyesians, like a dolphin undulating in the water. Rather like butterfly stroke but smoother. He cooked us all fish on an open fire on an islet and served salad and rice to go with it and water from containers he brought to a motu from the boat.

Enjoyed my evening in the complete luxury of my room and slept peacefully.

The next day I had to move out because the room had been available for only one night. I found a room at the dilapidated and rickety Bora Bora Yacht Club. Although the bed was surrounded by a mosquito net hanging from the ceiling it was full of dozens of small holes at various places in the netting. A whole squadron of flying needles would easily get inside. The windows were the normal wooden type. Unlike other places I've stayed the sea does not here lap gently on a sandy shore. It smashes itself loudly against the sea wall making the bed and floor reverberate.

I meet Jane and Chris Francis and their two children. They are anchored nearby. They do school lessons on the boat with their children for three hours a day most days. This can't be easy to accomplish when the weather is rough. Two years ago they set sail from Essex and are heading for Australia. We all walk into the small town of Vaitape together and back. They thoughtfully invited me to join them on their boat for dinner, which I accepted. Their boat is called 'Norn' and they are friends of the couple on 'Dapper Dan'.

Jane, like the majority of women I met sailing with their partners, does not enjoy the sailing life. She would much rather have a proper house of stone or brick rather than living on a small, cramped boat enduring frequent bad weather.

At a quarter past six the next morning I left the yacht club and walked the few minutes to the ferry. The pale peach glow of dawn was just peeping over the horizon. The morning was an eggshell blue and the air fresh and cool. It was silent accept for the sound of the soft waves here gently massaging the shore.

The ride back was uncomfortable as the boat crashed into the high swell. About 20 per cent of the passengers were sea sick. The ferry rose up on tall waves then dropped with a crash into the troughs.

Chapter Eleven

At last I am going to be free! I am excited to be moving out of my guest house to stay at the Tiare Tahiti hotel on the sea front in Papeete. The hotel only opened eight months before and is in spick and span condition. The rooms are simple: no fridge, bar or coffee making machine. Perhaps they don't want to use too much electricity. It is clean and there are no insects. It is a real hotel.

I plan to move into the hotel in two days time. I leave a message at Maeva boat dock for Thierry telling him I am moving at noon on Friday and could he please help. It's not so much the bags or travel into the town that I would like Thierry's help with, I fear the reaction of Mr Paris when I tell him I want to move out. He is a bad-tempered man with no qualms about being rude or aggressive to a female.

On Friday all my packing is done and I've cleaned my room. No phone call to the guest house from Thierry and no sign of him. I feel very strongly that Mr Paris and his family will physically block me from leaving if I go to them now. He will say I must pay another two weeks rent for the remainder of the original booking of a month. But it hasn't been as I expected or as I was told and I want to go early.

They hardly cleaned my room, they didn't provide breakfast fruit as promised and they rarely included me in anything. I telephone the Pleutins but there is no reply.

I'm beginning to feel trapped and worried. The hill is too steep and the temperature is too high for me to carry my three bags a mile down the hill to the bus stop. It is more a track than a road down between houses, banana trees and many loose dogs.

I decide to walk to the gas station, without my belongings, and ask them to telephone a taxi to collect me and my belongings from the guest house. They are kind and they do so. The taxi has to come from Papeete so it will take half an hour to arrive. I wait at the gas station where I meet a French Tahitian man, Serge. He works there and speaks good English. We chat and in the course of that I explain my predicament. I ask if he would kindly come with me to give in my notice, just for moral support and so that Mr Paris will not be able to bully me so easily as he would if I was alone. Also if Mr Paris is not there then there are several family members living there to whom I could give notice but they don't understand English so perhaps Serge could translate my notice giving to them. He agrees.

As Serge and I travel up the remote hill in the taxi the taxi driver is muttering 'tis terrible, tis terrible. Not good for you here. Not good. Terrible. Terrible.'

At the guest house Serge explains to Mrs Paris and her grandson that I am checking out immediately. Within three minutes Mr Paris comes out to us. We are standing in the garden. Behind us sheets are blowing in the breeze. Mr Paris takes us to his small office to give me a receipt. His face is dark and full of rage.

'I am now paying one night of fee, for tonight, even though I will not be here and I will pay the telephone charges and that will bring me up to date,' I say

Mr Paris says, as expected, 'You really should pay at least one week more because I have turned people down. I could have other people here but I told them I was full.'

'You are not full. There are six cabins and they are all empty except for the one I was in. There is not a single other person staying here. You have plenty of room.'

His face is grim, his mouth like the metal jaws of an animal trap just as I'd anticipated. But he didn't want to lose face and be seen to bully a woman in front of someone from a local business.

He asked where I would be staying in case there were telephone calls or mail. I told him. Then Serge and I put my belongings in the taxi. A bag of clothes, a bag of books and notebooks and a bag of food. We stop at the gas station for Serge to go back to work. I thank him profusely. I offer him money which he refuses. I offer him fruit which he refuses. I am so very grateful to him for his help that I say I would like to repay his kindness. 'Your smile is enough,' he says grinning.

The hotel in Papeete is owned by a friendly, intelligent, young Japanese couple. They know big Ata and laugh at my calling him 'BIG Ata' because they acknowledge yes, he is big! The husband of the couple does business with Ata because the husband also owns pearl farms and sells pearls in Japan.

At six o'clock on my first morning at the hotel I met Thierry who'd left a message for me to say let's have coffee and try to call Plainsong and Manana on the radio. There were designated times when they knew we would try to call. It often didn't work and the signal didn't get through. Thierry explained that he and his girlfriend had gone to stay for a few days at a friend's house so he was away from the boat when I left my message. By the time he was back he found I'd left the guest house. We went to his boat and tried to call the other boats way south by now. All quiet. No response. Thierry was taking some friends to the airport because they were moving back to France. I went back to town.

Wandering around the indoor market I pass the fruit and fish and vegetables on the ground floor. There are no mangos yet as it is not the season for another month. There are many papaya, bananas and lemons. There is breadfruit both cooked and uncooked and taro which is a root vegetable that looks rather like turnip and must be cooked before eating.

Upstairs are simple souveniers: tee shirts, small wooden tiki (warrier gods), carved wooden bowls and many shells, loose or made into necklaces and bracelets. The islands have no metals or gems. What they do have are shells and fish, fruit and flowers and these they share. It is common to see both men and women wearing a flower behind their ear.

Visited Cyberspace to check messages and had many. Francis had sent six short messages then a long one detailing his visit to Pitcairn Island with Chris Chan in bad weather. Winds were blowing between 40 and 50 knots. There were no safe anchorages so they could not land. Astonishingly, the church minister on the island and his wife spoke by radio to Francis and Chris, Francis's crew, and the unbelievable part was that he and Chris had been at school together and hadn't spoken to each other for 30 years until now!

Plainsong moved on because of the gales and weathered two full days of atrocious weather, suffering some minor damage including ripped sails and the blade of the ever faithful wind vane sheering off. I knew there was a spare on board, though it couldn't be attached until the weather was settled. The last message said the weather was bright and calm.

I sent a message back and replied to other messages. That evening having a fruit juice and a chat in the sitting area of the hotel near reception a man called Vince was telling me about his work building boats. He was also a guest in the hotel. He was slim and rugged and drank a local beer.

'I'm from New Zealand but live in Perth. Great country, Australia. I build boats anywhere in the world,' he said. He builds aluminium boats. Fishing boats, small or large, ferries, sailboats. He has a team of designers and builders who work for him. He is in Tahiti drumming up business and getting contracts.

'Your wife must miss you when you are away,' I say.

'She knows the most important thing in my life is to build boats and I'll go wherever I have to, to do it.'

Later, a young man friend of the receptionist was talking excitedly about his new job. He was 23 and was going to be a finance director covering all of Asia for a large company manufacturing small household items. He had lived in Tahiti for four months.

'Will you miss Tahiti,?' I ask

'Ah,' he sighed. 'The women, yes." He grinned, his eyes lit up and his face softened with memories. 'They just give themselves to you, quickly, unexpectedly, because you don't know them well. You just meet them and talk with them and within an hour or two they just lean against my body, they press themselves against me and kiss me. Then they want sex. They tell me that. Many do not understand that it is unhealthy to have unprotected sex. I always insist on using condoms but one woman she refused. She said to me 'Look how clean and healthy I am.'She refused to have sex if I used a condom so I refused to have sex at all."

"Sex is just like a meal to them," he said. "It is like food. They feel like some so they go and get it. It is not special and favours are freely given. So as you can imagine," he continued, "to men from other places this is a sexual paradise.'

As I thought about what he said it was understandable

Papeete, Tahiti

now why so many men jumped ship and why there was that mutiny on the Bounty. What beguiles the men is the combination of several things at once : beautiful sensual women, lush, luxuriant green mountains growing bananas, mangos, papaya, grapefruit and other fruits, coconuts to drink, fish for catching inside and outside the lagoon so that having enough to eat is easy and one can live in almost self-sufficiency. There is very little that needs to be bought.

In the warm to hot climate it is essential not to wear many clothes just shorts and a top or scrap of cotton to wrap around the body. There are no freezing or icy winds. Then to top it all there is the free and easy sex life. Women visiting the islands adore the beauty and the fruit and don't seem fixated on the sex. But for men? What more could a guy want?

31st August and I am back in Bora Bora. This time I flew in on a little propeller plane. I slept until two in the morning and woke feeling refreshed. Went outside onto the terrace of a nice place where I was staying. I wanted to look at the stars. Time and the heavens had moved on. Scorpio and the Southern Cross were not up yet.

There was the soft whisper of wavelets caressing the beach with the occasional barely perceptible rustle of leaves and palm fronds in the still air. I felt very happy and at one with life. I thought of Francis and Chris battling the elements on their way to Chile and the roaring 40s and the screaming 50s latitudes and smiled in the darkness. I was so glad I was here and not with them.

Early morning I rented a bicycle for the day and went for a ride of discovery. I learned that The Bora Bora Hotel was the first hotel on the island and Moana Adventure Tours was set up at the same time to take hotel guests on lagoon excursions. They still have the exclusive contract with the hotel. There was little road traffic so it was carefree bicycling around and stopping wherever I wanted to drink in the view.

When I get back to the hotel I sit on the terrace drinking tea. Two female guests are chatting in French. The middle-aged owner comes over to chat to me. I ask how it is that his hair is blonde and curly and not dark like other Polynesians. He tells me it is because his grandmother was from the Cook Islands and there it is not unusual. I stand to look into the sea watching the little blue fish.

"You are so fair," he says. "I don't know if you are a ghost, or a woman or a dream." Suddenly he has scooped me up across his arms and is running with me into the sea.

"Put me down," I struggle. "Put me down."

He laughs. "No, I want to see if you are real or a vision." He is still moving and then we are in deep water. I shriek.

"I don't like the deep water, take me back."

He laughs again and carries me back towards the terrace. I slip from his arms into the shallow water and walk to the terrace. We both laugh. He had followed a spontaneous urge for fun. He has gone quickly ahead and disappears into the building reappearing with a towel. He hands it to me.

"You can take off your wet swimsuit."

"No, I can dry myself with it on."

"Take it off. I've seen lots of women. I've seen it all. Nakedness is not new." The two women on the terrace listen and watch and shrug their shoulders smiling.

"Well, I'll keep it on for now." I dry myself a little and go to my room to shower and put on shorts and a top. A short time later back on the terrace the owner smiles and says he didn't mean to frighten me. I realize that he was being playful and meant no harm. "I know," I say. "Tell me about your life here," and we all listen.

Just before dusk as a few guests are chatting together on the terrace two French women come over to me and speak to me in English. "We have bad news. Terrible news. You must sit down." My heart jumps to my mouth. Francis and Chris are lost. Something has happened to them or my family. Time slows. "Princess Diana has died. It was a traffic accident in Paris. It's just been on the news." Thank God Francis and Chris are okay is my first thought. Then I think what an odd thing to happen. That a young, beautiful and vibrant woman should die suddenly is a shock. Yet it is only odd because it is royalty. When a person is famous or rich or both they can appear lucky. They appear to have Teflon coating against the bad things of life. That is why it is so surprising if a terrible tragedy occurs to them. I think of all the traffic accidents and sudden deaths that occur around the world where loved ones try to cope and fathom out how their lives have changed. The two women look at me sad for me and worried that I will cry. "How very sad. Awful for her two boys. And for the rest of her family," I say. I wonder how you tell children their mother or father isn't there anymore. I'd have to say they are still there in the sky looking down. The idea they are just not there, that they are gone completely is too hard to accept. I sit feeling relieved nothing bad has happened to Francis and Chris and at the same time shocked that someone so young and full of life should die in a dreadful accident. They tell me what they have heard on the radio. There are no televisions in the hotel and only one shared small radio in the kitchen tuned to a local station. Life is so beautiful and yet so fragile.

Death can be so sudden and unexpected. Any one of us can disappear from living. The realization of how tenuous our thread to life is makes me appreciate it. It makes me think it is all the more important to give praise where it is deserved, to think and do good where one can and to hold hands, to kiss on the cheek, and to hug those we care about, whoever they are. Perhaps I can learn from the Polynesians who have a good attitude to being mellow, relaxed and enjoying the moment.

On Sunday I bicycled to Viatape, the only town on the island though in truth little more than a village. It has a post office, a dozen or so tiny shops and a small landing stage. Most of the village shops are closed on Sundays here and across the island. It has two churches, one Protestant and one Catholic.

I followed the sound of music into the Catholic church. It was good though I did not stay. There was a strange unwelcome juxtaposition of the lovely, lively, warm, enthusiastic, relaxed Polynesians and the solemn, dour, self-important clergymen dragging down any show of feelings of joy.

For over a hundred and fifty years the Church, by that I mean all the churches, clamped down and banned all music on all the islands in Polynesia. No music, no dancing, no singing. Except for that allowed in church. The missionaries thought too much music, singing and dancing would lead to sex and that would be a bad thing. Well, they got that wrong because the Polynesians never lost or postponed their delight and sense of fun in having sex. Through all that one hundred and fifty years they copulated whenever they wanted, except perhaps in church!

Only in the 1950s did the societal rules loosen and the people began to re-discover their own cultural music, singing and dancing. They also began to wear comfortable clothes. The women no longer felt it necessary to wear dresses with high necks and long sleeves so unsuited and unhealthy in a hot environment.

The ride back to my newly discovered and very pleasant building of rented rooms was into the wind so it was hard work peddling.

I didn't have many days left so I went about exploring on the bicycle again. In the evening I went with Uta, a Japanese young woman also staying in the building, to a nearby hotel to watch a fire dance show.

It was the first time I had been out in the evening. It was pitch black so I used my small flashlight to guide us down the sandy, tree edged track to the hotel. In the distance we could see little dim lights from the water bungalows on stilts over the sea.

The show was on the sand next to the lagoon. Two canoes led the event, sailing 50 yards across the lagoon to the part where we were. The men shouted in Tahitian bearing flames just as they must have in the past. Half a dozen fit, muscular Polynesian men gave demonstrations of branches of fruit carrying and massive stone carrying. They used two weights of stone. One stone weighing close to 75 pounds and the other 200 pounds. No members of the audience volunteered to have a go after hearing the weight and seeing the maneuvering and effort necessary to lift each stone.

Then they twirled lighted batons over their head. It was interesting and spectacular to see their versatility as they spun the batons in front of them in circles, through their legs and behind their back with such speed that the air was filled with blue and yellow flames.

At night it is so peaceful in Polynesia that I want to stay awake and marvel at the universe. I almost always wake between 2 and 3 o'clock, then I read for an hour or two, and get up at half five to watch the dawn appear and clothe the sky in soft rainbow colour pastels. I am at Matira Point on Bora Bora where the sun rises above a long, very low motu. I go out of the communal kitchen through the French doors walking along the long terrace which is set in a sandy garden full of Plumeria – Frangipani trees and stand, drinking in the exotic scent, and gazing in admiration at the changing sky as the blindingly bright orb of sun slowly rises. The colours irridescent and pure. By eleven in the morning one feels the heat of the day. The sun bright, hot and rising high in the Southern sky and the shallow water and the sky are unbelievable blues yet they are real and I just wanted to lie there and look at them be part of them for all eternity.

At night a gentle breeze, the South East Trade Winds, blow and I hear what I thought was light rain but was actually the crackling of coconut fronds touching each other. Out in the dark is the distant muffled roar of the great ocean crashing against the reef and closer the soft trickle of water lapping the white sand outside my window.

It is a gentle life, both the climate and, modernly, the people. Never did I hear a Polynesian voice raised in anger, other voices yes, but not Polynesian.

Wednesday, 3rd September. I leave my Bora Bora accommodation at half five in the morning in a mini-bus. Just the female driver and me head for the ferry that will take me across the lagoon to the small airport.

It is still dark with a gentle light creeping into the sky. The blue lagoon is calm. A few ripples shyly hug the shore while in the distance the creamy white foam folds itself over the barrier reef.

Half a dozen colourful small boats lie at anchor, they are still in the morning silence that is broken only by our engine, the roosters crowing and the crackling of palm fronds.

After three months living amongst these Polynesian islands and its people I realize I don't want to leave this calmness and beauty. Yet I have another life and must rejoin it.

Life in these islands is unhurried, except for the golden brown mother hens dashing across the road with their fluffy lemon coloured chicks. Men and women often commute by rowing in canoes. Several times a year they have celebrations which include canoe races. Both men and women wear flower garlands in their hair at these times. The sun rises over the green, lush mountainous island of Moorea opposite my anchorage in Tahiti. The gentle sound of men singing in the evening and also some early mornings as we eat breakfast of thick skinned grapefruit and tea and toast on deck. Singing simply for the joy of life. Sounds of the sea pounding against the reef a thousand feet away has lessened overnight. Now there is just the soft sound of surf washing against the coral. A grey heron sits expectantly on a post waiting for breakfast. On shore a few small plumes of grey smoke drift up in the still air.

French Polynesia will remain special, like a beloved that is treasured and remembered and carried always in one's heart. The Marquesas, the Tuamotus, and the Tahitian Islands will be often in my thoughts, especially on bitter, cold rainy days. But there on any day, the memory will be like a flame to warm me and make me smile.

In my mind it will always be a land where curling smoke rises slowly from small fires near homes, where the people are strong and independent and where, in the darkness of evening, under the mango trees, men sing songs deep and slow into the night.

Chapter Twelve

Buenos Aires, Argentina

An hour after dawn, as the plane flew over South America from England, the thick layers of cloud dispersed and it was possible to see a dry brown land which looked greener near the coast and rivers. The shapes of the estuaries were sharp and spiny as they cut through the ground to run to the ocean. Like hard, cold steel the rivers glinted in the morning light and at times when the sun hit them they sparkled brightly like silver.

The Spanish explorers called the region Argentina from the Latin for silver, argentum though they did not know that although the country had many minerals silver was not abundant. It seems they could have named it because of the silver coloured water of the River Plate (Rio de la Plata). It is the confluence of the Uruguay River and the Parana river that open out into a gulf facing the Atlantic. From the plane it is easy to see why it was given that name.

I headed to my hotel in an airport bus which rapidly passed the door of my hotel, the driver refusing to agree to my request to stop and let me off there. No, he said, the only stop is the terminus. At the busy terminus I got a taxi the few miles to my hotel.

The suitcase was heavy with boat equipment including two large and heavy winch handles, four heavy steel shackles and a replacement wind gauge. I had bought them in London and was taking them to our boat in Ushuaia, Argentina, down near Cape Horn. Wheels on the suitcase made it easy except, of course, going up or down stairs.

The taxi stopped after two miles in a deserted area of empty warehouses and offices. It was a weekend. There was no traffic and no people. The driver turned to me as I sat in the front passenger seat and took my hand for what I thought must be a greeting. "I read energy," he said. "You are married and your husband is a cold man."

I knew he was making this up based on the fact I was travelling alone without a husband as chaperone.

"It is best to read energy if I put my hand here," he said placing his hand on my stomach. His hands looked the size of hams. He looked fit and in his forties. I looked into the rear view and wing mirrors. No-one around. If I screamed he might attack me, if I jumped from the car and ran I was afraid that because he was bigger than me and fit if he caught me he might attack me more severely for running away. I considered making a run for it and kicking him in the balls if he caught me but the odds weren't good that I could get away. If he wanted to he could simply snap me like a twig. I thought I'd better play along and cajole him into taking me to the hotel, or at least to where there were other people.

A small woman against a large man might not win a physical fight but she very well might win in a battle of wits.

"If you don't mind," I said, removing his hand. "Please don't put your hand on my stomach."

"Okay. I would like to teach you the tango" .

"I would really like to go to my hotel now. It has been a very long flight of thirteen hours and I've been awake for twenty four hours. I'm very tired. Please take me to the hotel so that I can sleep."

"Okay, of course," he said driving away as if nothing strange had happened.

Within eight minutes we were at the hotel. "Here is my number, he said. If you or your husband need anything in Buenos Aires just let me know. You are a very special lady." Sure, right, I thought.

Two hours later he was back at the hotel to take me to learn tango, so he told the hotel manager. The hotel manager was prepared because I'd told him I wasn't available for any callers and not to give my room number out or my name. He was back at nine o'clock after breakfast but the manager saw him off again.

The following day I explored the big, bustling city with its mixture of architecture from nineteenth century to the present. It was a fabulous mix of older Spanish and French ornate stone buildings and modern glass skyscrapers. I watch dramatic sexy tangos in the area La Boca.

For the most part the city looked tired and worn, as did many of the people. Their shoes worn down, dull and unpolished. On Avenue Cordoba there were two busy shoe shine stalls but it didn't change the overall look of most of the shoes.

The majority of people walking by were dark haired, dark eyed with short bodies and they picked their way along cracked pavements. The high inflation had obviously effected the city.

It is unfortunate that the USA government is so anti-socialist. It kicks out hard and automatically against those who want to have a national free health care system or protect resources of water, electricity or manufacturing or otherwise care for its population.

George W Bush and the IMF took a hard line against

Argentina when it needed help for its banks. Argentina is a great country with wide, varied natural resources and a well developed economy especially for exports of its beef and cereals. It is odd that it needed to go to the IMF. Do stock market traders interfere with its assets? Argentina has 86 million acres of arable land, it grows cotton, sugar, fruit, wheat and barley. It makes delicious wine. It grows flax for linseed oil and makes honey. It has 50 million cattle, 95 million chickens and three and a half million horses. It is well known for breeding racing and polo horses. It is puzzling.

Inflation in 1975 was 300% then in 1983-5 it was 900%.

Landline communication distribution was very slow with only 220 landlines for every 1,000 people in 2003. At the same time there were 180 mobile phones for every 1,000 people. In 2015 the number of mobiles had grown to 31 million. 84% of the adult population had a mobile phone. This is a good thing for everyone. Regardless of what stories they are fed by conglomerates people can now share more easily their own views and stories : Older people can be in touch with others and young people can learn about the world and decide how they want their world to be.

In 2001 Argentina had five Presidents within a two week period. All Argentina needs is good Government with no outside interference.

Two days later I enjoyed a five and a half hour bus ride to Mar del Plata about two hundred miles south. On the edge of the city live the poorest people in one or two roomed corrugated metal homes. Some are brick and some a mixture of both. Horses grazed on poor land where posse notices hang across fences.

A stream runs along the road for over a hundred miles and as it goes further from the city the landscape becomes open and wild. It is flat pampas with clumps of trees in the distance breaking the horizon. Streams and rivers curve across the grassland. Egrets stand fishing and hawks sit on posts waiting for the right movement. Some fields are so full of water they look like swamps. Closer to Mar del Plata the land looks fertile with crops and cattle.

Argentina, a country of hunky, macho gauchos on elegant horses crossing the open grassland pampas. A place where most of the best polo ponies and players come from. A place of llamas and alpacas.

A woman sitting beside me on the bus asked if I was a tourist and if I was alone. In broken Spanish I said I was to both questions. Then she asked if I had a hotel booking. (This was before the internet and I hadn't got a booking.) Our conversation was difficult because she spoke no English and I had few words of Spanish however with my Spanish dictionary between us she said she would take me to the information desk at the coach station and would look through the list of hotels to select the best for me.

At the information desk she had the attendant ring the selected hotels. Four of them were full. The fifth had space and was good and safe in her opinion. Then she pointed to the nearby taxi rank, said goodbye, gave me a hug and was gone. I was very lucky to have met her.

The reason for being in Mar del Plata was to check out the storage and cleaning facilities for our boat once she'd been around Cape Horn and come up to this area. She would have a clean and an equipment check up before going on up to Brazil.

The town was founded by rich Buenos Aires residents in the 1800s and by the 1930s it had become a busy Atlantic resort. It is a straggly town with the brown Atlantic rolling in and being broken up by concrete fingers extending 30 feet into the Ocean. It is the most popular Argentine resort with a resident population of approximately 400,000 and over two million visitors during the summer.

Both Yacht Club Argentina and Club Nautico were friendly, helpful and had good facilities. Club Nautico was just then lowering a sailboat unto the water using huge slings slung under her hull.

On the bus back to Buenos Aires the next day, as we drew close to the terminus, the woman in the seat next to mine asked if I was on the bus solo and when I said yes she told me to please be careful and to hold my bag securely and watch the areas I walked in.

On my last day in Buenos Aires I planned to visit the Museum of Beautiful Art, then the Recoleta Cultural Centre. Alas, both of them were closed in the morning and not opening until two o'clock.

I visited the Church of Pila, Our Lady of Pilar Basilica. Built in the 1700s it has remained popular. It is painted white inside and out with huge arched niches containing elaborate sculptures in gold leaf. The walls and ceilings are smooth white, without the bright yellow and orange paint of Mexico or the intricate carved wood of Britain, Italy or France. An enormous solid silver seven foot long chest serves as the alter table. It is stunning in its shining metal and embossed detail. Behind it are marble pillars the colour of coffee and of pistachio ice cream. Around the edge of the church blue and yellow flower patterned tiles go from the floor to a height of three feet. The cloisters house the museum of various religious items including candlesticks, small boxes and figurines. The terracotta tiled floor is clean and worn and the whole church has a happy feeling and of peace and security. The sound of Gregorian chant softly filled the air.

Cemeteries are not places high on my list of must see sites. However, I heard that the cemetery here was brilliant so I went outside to explore.

No grassy lawns with headstones met my eyes. Instead I saw avenues of crypts. It was like a village with the houses closely packed together yet all different in design. Some had cupolas, some a cross, some a doorway and all with the family name carved into the marble at eye level. Suddenly a man who worked there gently took my elbow, "you want to see Evita's tomb? he asked in Spanish.

I had not known Evita Peron's tomb was there but I was keen to see it. He gave me directions down, then turn then turn again and off I went. I got lost and couldn't find it for some time. Then I noticed a crypt scattered with flowers and walked towards it. There it was " Eva Duarte". Duarte! Her family name. I had been looking for Peron. Here was a woman whose ability to connect with the masses helped her husband become a successful President of Argentina. Sadly Eva became ill and died aged only 33. A wrought iron gate was in the centre lovingly filled with single flowers pushed through the curling patterns of the railing. There was a sunflower and pink and red roses and carnations. This was a person that the people still loved.

The man who had spoken to me earlier asked me to sign the visitors book as I was leaving. A Japanese man who had been taking photographs of Eva's tomb was taking his last photographs of the cemetery. His entry said "I only came to Argentina to see Evita's tomb".

Just before I hurried out into the pouring rain the cemetery assistant bent down, kissed me quickly on the left cheek and wished me "Felice Navidad".

With a city map held over my head I hurried to the Art Museum. What a museum! It is marvellous. Museo Belle Artes.

Gorgeous large sensitive Augustus Rodin sculptures and a plaster copy of The Kiss. The four originals are in The Tate Gallery, London (though it goes on loan around Britain to various galleries); in Paris, Philadelphia, and Copenhagen.

Also on display is the most beautiful painting by Gaugin

I have seen. It is "Vahine no te Miti" "Woman by the sea". There is something gentle in it that is not often seen in his other paintings. On the woman's right knee rests her sarong or paraeu made of exactly the same colour and pattern still worn in Polynesia today.

The European and Argentine sections have good paintings under excellent lighting.

Feeling happy and artistically well-fed I decided that before going back to the hotel I would stop to see the Palace of Justice (or Tribunales). It is a stunning building with towering arches and great doorways. Courts are monuments to fairness and balance. An aim of law is to keep physical violence out of disagreements. But the respect for courts disappeared somewhat when I returned to my hotel and read that two judges had been prosecuted for taking bribes to make sure a case went a particular way.

Some judges do not realise the importance of integrity. It is fundamental to their position in society. They should not act for money, influence or self-agrandisement instead they should be selfless for what is legally right in both equity and black letter law. If all lawyers, including judges do not do that then people will lose respect for the whole institution of law and their lies cynicism and chaos.

President Peron had done enormous good for his country. He legitimized trade unions, secured voting rights for women and made university education available to those capable of achieving high levels of understanding. But outside forces seemed to have become involved in his overthrow.

In the square outside the Palace of Justice were outlines of bodies drawn on the ground, like those in crime programmes where there is a thick, white chalk outline of where a body lay. Most had names written next to them. I took photographs of them and wondered what they were only to give myself a jolt that evening sitting in my hotel room when I read that they were reminders to the Government of the thousands of "disappeareds".

In 1955 Juan Peron the leader of Argentina was forced out of office by the military. Many coups from the 1950s onwards in South America were said to be encouraged or led by the USA. The USA also allegedly heavily influenced the media to print false stories about good politicians. Peron was elected on his policies to increase the pay of agricultural and industrial workers and to improve health care. In 1973 Peron returned to office but died a year later. Inflation ran at a fast and harmful pace going up from an eye-watering 300 % in 1975 to painful 900% in 1985.

Argentina was not alone in being subject to outside interference allegedly by the USA. Chile also suffered from destablisation when the USA sent in operatives to create unrest. Once again a country had a leader who wanted to improve the basic living conditions of the majority of the population. Salvador Allende wanted to help his people. He won the election in 1970. In 1972 inflation was 150%. The USA maintained an aggressive anti-Allende stance. It was reported that notes between a CIA official and Nixon say that the USA should make the Chile economy scream in order to destroy the government.

It arranged that not a nut or bolt would be sent to Chile which meant that within a few years a third of all its buses and trucks were off the road because they could not get the parts to repair the vehicles. In 1975 Allende was deposed and is said to have shot himself.

Back in Argentina during the dirty war cars without number plates during those difficult turbulent years would abduct people from the street and they were never seen again. Many were tortured. All those missing were believed to have been murdered. One time three nuns were taken and thrown out of an aircraft over the Atlantic. This, I learned, was not an isolated incident. Many people were drugged and callously and traumatically thrown out of planes. Between 1976 and 1983 this dirty war took place and it is said up to 30,000 people were murdered by the military. The victims included students and people who sympathised and supported socialism. Even pregnant women were taken, given time to have the child then the child given away to a right wing supporter and the mother killed.

Every Thursday the mothers of the disappeared marched in the square opposite the Presidential Palace, together with the Grandmothers of the disappeared, wanting to know what happened to their children and grandchildren. The mothers wanting to show the death of their child would not be forgotten and the Grandmothers wanting to know where their grandchild was – the child allowed to be born before their mother killed. These were called Las Madres de Plaza de Mayo and Las Abuelas de Plaza de Mayo.

In such countries where the rule of law has not operated the people are suspicious of authority and have seen and are marked by the raw evil of a corrupt Government. Over time some of these countries will have leaders the people can trust and who will truly be guardians of the society.

Epilogue: Navy Captain Scilingo acknowledged in 2005 on trial in Spain being charged under the Human Rights Convention that he threw, or arranged to have thrown, political prisoners alive but drugged out of planes over the Atlantic. He was sentenced to a total of 1,084 years in prison.

Argentina has recently become more aligned with South America and paid off all debts to the IMF.

Brazil is suffering anti-socialist de-stabalisation and the socialist government attacked by what is said to be fabricated allegations of corruption.

Chapter Thirteen

Patagonia

The three and a half hour flight from Buenos Aires to Ushuaia travelled over hundreds of miles of pampas until the lower part of the Andes came into view.

Snow capped crags and ice fields led to the Beagle Channel where multi-coloured houses out of a children's book pressed together for warmth.

I was down in Ushuaia to go sailing. First, before Plainsong arrived, I was keen to see a bit of the town and especially the Maritime Museum.

This must be one of the best seafaring museums anywhere with fabulous charts. An especially interesting one was one dated 1519 by Lopo Homem of Europe and South America which Ferdinand Magellan used to sail around south America and through the channel that separates Tierra del Fuego from the mainland.

The area got its name from the fires lit by the natives who even lit little fires in the confines of their small boats. The first explorers with Magellen called it the Land of smoke because from sea the men saw the smoke rising in many places, Tierra del Fuego - though now it often translated as Land of Fire. The climate is teeth chattering cold, in winter usually zero degrees centigrade and in summer ten degrees. The wind often blows at sixty knots yet the people who live here are happy.

Magellan went through the channel in 1520 and by 1530 there were very good charts produced by the Mercator chart makers. Gerardus Mercator made his map of the earth for mariners in 1569. This helped them to navigate even though countries further from the poles are distorted. Mercator's maps are still important and form the basis for maps on the web and mapping Mars by NASA. Further mapping of the earth by John Snyder used Mercator as the basis of his mapping extending it using Landsat data and by developing a complex system on top of it called the Space Oblique Mercator Projection.

At the museum I notice in the corners of the charts are lovely drawings. Some have cherubs blowing the wind around the earth, some have a boat sailing in a bay between mountains.

I feel sorry for the artist James Whistler, who, over three hundred years after these early charts, was sacked by the American Survey Department for habitually drawing birds on the charts he had been hired to draw. They did not want any special flourishes. Still, their loss was our gain because he went on to produce moving, evocative paintings and drawings including along the River Thames and of Venice.

Why is there no famous island, town or river called Elcano, or Sebastian, after Sebastian Elcano of Spain? He started out in one of the ships with Magellan. Magellan's adventure left Spain with five ships and two hundred and twenty six men but only the ship "Victoria" manned by Elcano and seventeen men managed to return to Spain, doing so on 6th December, 1522.

Magellan was one of those who did not make it home. He was killed in the Philippines. There can be no denying that Sebastian Elcano was a great sailor.

Elcano, Magellan and Francis Drake were investigating these waters almost five hundred years ago. The weather here is changeable and often rough with almost constant low temperatures and snow falls most of the year. Those sailors came to this far flung area not knowing what food they would find, if any, or whether there was fresh water and braving strong currents, wild winds and jagged rocks to find a passage to the Pacific Ocean.

One of the charts showed half submerged ships around Tierra del Fuego and Cape Horn. It covered the years from 1765 when the 'Purisima Conception', a Spanish vessel, sank to the year 1988 when 'Buque biblioteca Panameno' sank. There are eighty eight vessels listed.

There are beautiful wooden minature boat models exhibited of ships such as 'The Beagle', the 'Allen Gardiner', the 'Romanche Trinidad' (Magellan's ship) and the 'Duchess of Albany' (from Liverpool). The models were made by Miron Gonik, an engineer living in Argentina.

A telephone call came for me at the hotel. Plainsong has arrived in Puerto Williams in Chile but can't sail upwind to Ushuaia . It was suggested I get a taxi for a journey just over an hour to Almanza. So I got my bags and off I went.

The journey was over a rough, pot-holed, lumpy track through woods and fields. At times the track was a muddy squelchy bit of ground through stands of trees. There were no houses anywhere. There were no buildings of any sort. The driver said it was like rally car driving as we skidded about.

There was only one boat at the small wooden, naval office pontoon, our boat, 'Plainsong'. The population is less than thirty and some of these belong to the navy. The naval officers at Almanza, Argentina, keep their peepers peeled for any incursions from Puerto Williams which is in Chile.

At different stages of the journey Francis had various members of crew. There was just one aboard now, the others having flown home. Francis had to check in there because he had sailed from Puerto Williams, Chile, to Almanza, which is, like Ushuaia, in Argentina.

Within two hours we were off again down the Beagle Channel to Puerto Williams for an overnight stay there where it was more sheltered from the wind.

Puerto Williams is a pretty, green bay with a small population of less than two thousand. The place is small and enclosed with trees clumping together on the lower hillsides with snow capped mountains beyond. The pier was a small sunken ship. To get ashore for a walk we tied up to another sailboat which was tied to the ship. We jumped across to the sailboat, then up a ladder to the ship's deck, across the wide deck and then jumped onto the land.

We walked in that damp, cold air that chills through jackets, through skin so that ones very veins feel frozen. It did make the cabin feel warm once we were back there and putting the kettle on.

Puerto Williams is the most southerly town in the world and lies on the Isla Navarino. Ushuaia is the most southerly city, though its population is around fifty thousand and is on the southern part of Tierra del Fuego opposite Navarino.

Two days later when the wind had moderated we set sail for Ushuaia. Another crew member would meet us there and they would sail around Cape Horn for fun and adventure. Not my scene!

The new crew member, Brian, was actually the boat builder who built Plainsong in his Tideways boatyard in Salcombe, Devon from a mold from Bloncel designed by John Rock. While building the yacht interior for Francis

Brian had become a good friend. He was a lovely guy, relaxed, always upbeat and a good sailor. Within half an hour of leaving Puerto Williams the sea was rough as the wind picked up to twenty and twenty five knots and came from ahead bashing into the prow of the boat making it a very uncomfortable and wet seven hour sail journey.

Anticipating a good hot meal at about seven o'clock that evening it soon became clear there was no way this was going to happen. First the sails had to be uncleated, folded and stowed. This took a long time. The gas for cooker ran out but wasn't replaced until the sails were put away. Then the Tilly lamp, which gave such a warm glow and some warmth to the cabin, ran out of kerosene, then its mantle broke and had to be replaced. We ate dinner at nine o'clock.

Little sailing got done in this part of South America because of the sea conditions. Francis and his crew set off a few days later to round Cape Horn, a lifetime dream. Then they would sail up to Mar del Plata. I went on to England to find a place to live for when the sailing adventure was over and I moved my things from California to England. There was a window of time to do this before meeting up with Francis again in Brazil.

Chapter Fourteen

Florianopolis, Brazil

Eating papaya and drinking caipirinhas - sugar cane brandy cocktails - in Brazil wasn't exactly what I had in mind when I left Los Angeles. All I knew then for sure was that we were going to have adventures and fun, with occasional gales!

We would sail from Florianopolis, a big, bustling beach city in the south, to Rio and then travel to the African influenced city of Salvador in the north.

It is amazing to realise Brazil is approximately 3,319, 662 sq miles. It is larger than the USA (excluding Alaska) and larger than Australia. It has the world's largest rivers, tropical forest, wetlands and an extraordinary diversity of plants and animals. The Atlantic coastline runs for four thousand five hundred miles. Over to the west the Iguacu falls, the mightiest waterfall on the Continent roars and rushes for two miles along the Argentina border inside National Parks. More Japanese people live in Brazil than anywhere else outside of Japan. It has one of the largest African communities outside Africa.

It has 3 time zones the main one of which is 3 hours

behind Greenwich Mean Time. The main one, covers most of the population and the most popular tourist cities, Rio, Sao Paulo and Santa Catarina.

Brazil is divided into 26 States from Rio Grande de Sul and Santa Catarina in the south to Amazonas, Amapa and Para in the north. It is a surprise to learn that snow can fall on the high ground in the southern states in their winter.

This is a country that sits happily on the equator that, in the north, has high humidity, heat and rainfall, with over 56,000 plant species yet 90% of its rainforest along the coast has been felled. 90% of the country lies in the tropical zone.

I flew out to Rio de Janeiro in July and two days later on to Florianopolis, where Francis and I had arranged to meet at the yacht club. Because there was not a connecting flight on the night I arrived in Rio, I stayed at the airport hotel for two nights. That would allow me a day of sightseeing in Rio and yet easy to check-in for the flight at six o'clock on the following morning. I am always excited in a new city to see how it looks from a window high above. I had so often stayed at airport hotels where I looked down on the twinkling city lights of offices, hotels and traffic lights at road intersections, sometimes my room even overlooked the runways. However, this time things didn't go as they normally do!

"Ronaldo, it is Alice" I said on the telephone from my room, after checking into my hotel on my first night in Rio.

"Ronaldo, my room is no good. I want a better room. It is seven o'clock at night and I want to see the lights of Rio," I explained to the hotel night manager. "I opened my curtains," I continued "and there is a wall. A wall. When I wake up in the morning I want to see Rio."

A laugh filled the telephone line. It was the manager. "We have a problem," he said.

"Yes, we do," I replied. "I want a room with a window." I had been astonished to discover that there were no windows in my room at all. It felt like a prison might. I didn't like it one bit.

"Well I have the solution."

"Good!"

"Don't open your curtains," he laughed again. I laughed too with a mixture of surprise and incredulity at his suggestion. Then I thought about the view or rather lack of view and spoke again.

"No that's not the best idea. I really do want a room with at least one window. You must have a room available you can give me."

"We have a problem," he said again.

"Yes, we have a problem."

"No, we really have a problem. You see none of our rooms have windows."

"What!

"None of our rooms have windows. You see we are in the middle of the airport terminal building so all the terminals and shops are around us. It is noisy and there is no view so we don't have windows."

"Oh! I see," I paused and thought quickly. "Okay then. I guess I'll get used to it."

A day later I flew from Rio down to Florianopolis. Many people in this Southern part of Brazil are of German and of Italian extraction. So many residents are of German descent that there is even a bierfest in the town of Blumenau during October, one of the biggest in the world, with Bavarian traditions. Florianopolis is a busy city partly on the mainland and including the island of Santa Catarina. With a population of close to a quarter of a million it sits below the Tropic of Capricorn. Once there was a political movement in the late 1900s to create a new country out of three States : Parana, Caterina, and Rio Grande Do Sul. It came to nothing.

To get to Florianopolis I had to change at the large

airport at Sao Paulo. There I was sent to baggage claim, immigration and customs. Immigration and customs were cleared two days before when I arrived in Brazil. Trying to explain this in badly broken Portuguese was not successful. I spent the next half hour jumping various check-in queues pointing to my departure time. With just ten minutes before departure I got to the right gate and on to my flight which luckily for me left twenty minutes behind schedule.

It was half ten in the morning and I been up since half past five. The airport bus had dropped me in the centre of town. I was standing in a street trying in vain to make a taxi driver understand I wanted to go to the yacht club. I even had the address written down so that if the taxi driver did not understand my bad Portuguese he would read it.

"What is your hotel?" he kept asking.

"No hotel," I reply. "I want to go to a boat in the marina." I can see he is thinking there are no cruise ships in so she cannot possibly want the harbour, this tiny slip of a woman cannot be going to a harbour, on her own, without her husband. He asks, "Where is your husband?" "On the boat" I tell him. He is puzzled. Just then, a well-dressed handsome man in his 40s appears at the driver's window next to me and asks the driver if he can help. He looks at me and in excellent, slightly accented English, he asks me where I would like to go. Surprised yet pleased at this intervention I tell him I have arrived to meet my husband on a sailboat at the harbour in the old city. He translates and smiles and waves as I am driven away.

The taxi driver chatters away in fast Portuguese so that I don't understand anything except the repeated use of the word "perigoso" for "dangerous"!

We pull up outside the small yacht club and as I pay the driver a voice says "Alice?" I look up surprised at the marina security man. He says my name again with a query. "Si,

Si" I reply. "You want Paco? Here he is," and he points and shouts to a tall, attractive broad, strong man in his 40s, hippy looking, with shoulder length dark, slightly graying curly hair who is standing a few feet away.

From recent messages from Francis I know that Paco is a terrific person and a bookseller from Mar del Plata, south of Buenas Aires who has joined him to sail up to Florianopolis. We shake hands and beam at each other. His face is wise and kind.

"Ola," I say. "Why are you here at the entrance? Is it co-incidence?"

"Yes, it is co-incidence. Francis and I knew you would arrive today but not your flight arrival time so we thought we would keep a look out."

"What a happy co-incidence you are here as I arrive," I say smiling as Paco insists on carrying my holdall. "Obrigada," I say in thanks. We see Francis rushing towards us grinning.

That evening the three of us enjoy a seafood dinner sitting in a courtyard filled with round tables in a cobbled piazza sharing stories while a good Brazilian band play lively music. There are about two hundred people enjoying the evening. There is something odd - I realize I am the only blonde.

Over the couple of days that Paco is with us we learn a little about politics in his home country, Argentina. Anyone who believes in a fair society, who appears to be socialist is in danger from right wing organisations. Five of his friends are amongst "The Disappeared ones". One of the baddies was someone Paco had known since they were both ten years old. Paco refused to meet or be in contact with him once he knew his role in the events of that time.

Paco leaves to go back to his book shop in Mar del Plata. Francis and I spend a day checking in with the Port Captain, several miles away, and with Immigration and Customs, whose office is in between our boat and the Port Captain.

We went to a money exchange bureau to change our Argentine money to Brazilian but they refused and said we should change it on the street! This was very peculiar because Argentinians are the biggest group of visitors to Brazil. Also there were six money changers shouting their trade on that street while two police officers stood nearby chatting and taking no notice.

Our guide book told us it was illegal to change money on the street yet we were told to do so by exchange bureau staff and it appeared to be a normal part of commerce.

We stocked up on fresh fruit and vegetables to supplement our many tins of food. The cauliflowers were enormous about two hand spans in diameter, less dense than the European variety and looking more like flowers resembling fat cow parsley. The apples were small and hard, the bananas small and firm with a delicious fragrance and the papaya huge, a foot long, with especially juicy orange flesh.

The day before departing we took a bus out to Praia de Joaquina, a long beach edged with sand dunes east of

Washing clothes in a bucket, Rio

Florianopolis. The dunes on this part of island are wonderfully tall and wide. In July, the winter, with temperature in the low 60s there was a cold, fast wind blowing in from the sea.

Although it was July I had forgotten it was winter. Strong easterly winds whipped through my thin, summer clothes. I walked with my arms crossed across my chest trying to keep the hard wind from freezing my body. White sea horses galloped on wave tops making this a super surfer spot. High waves crash on to the shore as the wind roars. On the way back we stopped again at the Port Captain's Office and then Immigration and Customs to check out. You cannot check out at the same time as you check in even though there might only be a few days between them and even though you know the date you will depart.

We set sail under the two bridges that join the island to the mainland leaving the skyscrapers of the city behind. Only an hour later the wind subsides so we motor. This was fortunate and unusual. It was fortunate because it allowed me to gain my sea legs. The sun shone and Florianopolis looked like any large city, miles of tall, ugly skyscrapers. We headed for the Bay of Magellan.

Life aboard. Being on a sailboat in Southern Brazil was not turning out as I had imagined. In my mind I had something like the climate of Southern California – light, gentle breezes with constant sunshine and a warm temperatures. Here in winter it is cool with cold winds and thin cottony grey clouds. Too cold to loll about or clean the boat wearing a swimsuit, especially when we are under way. I wore long johns, socks, a thick track suit over a thermal vest and sweater and then a life jacket. In a decent breeze and always on the open sea we habitually wear harnesses that are clipped to the jackstays to keep us attached to the boat should we lose our footing.

For the next four days we sail in fitful rain wearing oilskins and wellingtons. We see a pleasant village where we think we might walk and buy fish.

While strolling on shore a woman called Marilaine stops her car and gets out to chat with us. She wanted us to know that the people suffer. The politicians are corrupt and don't generally care about the people. At election time they feign interest and generosity but the rest of the time they are on the take – taking women, money and cocaine.

The little bay in which we are anchored has tidy, neatly painted houses dotted up a small hillside. There is a pretty turquoise house with yellow shutters and one in yellow with white shutters. There is one street with about forty houses facing the bay. I comment to Marilaine how prosperous the village looks. "Ah, yes," she laughs "most of the houses are weekend houses for the rich. The edge of the bay was cleared of poor housing some years ago and the poor were moved out of sight around the top of the hill. This better housing was built for visitors as holiday homes."

We motor a little further on to Porto Belo Yacht Club where we can peruse some local charts and get a weather forecast. Brazil doesn't seem to go in for marine forecasts. The Club is terrific and after obtaining the information we needed we sip mango juice and look out to the bay.

A huge thunderstorm swept over us on our fourth night and raged for about forty five minutes. The lightning was so bright that we couldn't sleep as it filled the sky. I lay terrified on my bunk imagining what would happen if it hit our metal mast. I visualized a misshapen boat and our charred remains. I kept my eyes closed but the lightning still penetrated. Every five minutes one of us would say "perhaps it's finished - no, perhaps not" as another crash and flash occurred. When it finally finished at two o'clock in the morning we fell into a deep sleep.

To Paranagua. It is Monday, 3rd August and by ten to six in the morning we have the anchor up and are away on a still clear morning. We leave Caixa d'Aco and then what looks like a huge town of skyscrapers that from our chart we figure out is Cambriou just before the port of Itajai. The eight foot high swell had now dissolved and we enjoyed the serenity of being at sea.

In a gentle breeze from the west we sail north. Later the wind became south east so we goose-winged comfortably along. There are mares' tails clouds to starboard with a dull blanket of cloud over the land and a sliver of moon shows in the daytime sky.

At lunchtime we see an albatross circling overhead. The huge wings so still in the air, its body white and plump. An hour later two penguins go by sitting in the water. The wind has picked up to 17 knots. Plainsong is steaming along close hauled at six knots in fifteen to seventeen knots of wind. This is Plainsong's top speed and one she doesn't often reach. There is one reef in the main.

It was nine o'clock at night and I was on watch. Clouds scud across the sky occasionally obscuring the silver moon. The air is sharp and cold, the sea dark and the sky inky. We took turns in the night to do three hour watches. We were headed for a place in Paranagua Bay. After ten o'clock at night the sea got busier. There were many small fishing boats. Some stationary and fishing, others travelling to their fishing ground. It was hard at times to make out whether they were moving or not and if they were moving which way were they going. Then some ships appeared all lit up like Christmas trees. I woke Francis up because our GPS position was falling too low on our compass course. The current may have been affecting us. There seemed to be too many ships to keep an eye on alone. Lights to our port side twinkle from the shoreline. Another problem was that there were two lights some distance off our port beam and I wasn't sure if they were heading towards us. The sea is very busy with boats of various sizes.

As we got closer to the river leading to the port we saw hundreds of lights, in clusters straight ahead and to the east looking like Blackpool illuminations. It seemed like lights on shore, a town perhaps. But according to the chart there was no land there.

We both kept a keen watch because there were the lights of several vessels in the vicinity. At one thirty I decided I really needed to sleep. As I lay in my sleeping bag I heard Francis call a ship over the radio giving the ship's course as identification and alerting it to our position. He told the ship our position, that we were immediately ahead of it and that our speed was five knots. Ships can see ships and other boats on their RADAR or if someone is keeping a look out they can spot small craft but at times nobody is looking out or looking at the equipment.

The ship's officer replied to say that they would pass on our starboard side and their speed was eighteen knots.

I got up again and stayed awake and on deck until half two. There were clumps of white lights stretching away ahead and to our right. We checked the charts again. So many lights puzzled us. We heard our friendly ship, the one that passed us to starboard, call the Port Office at Paranaqua informing them he hoped be at their office within two hours. The Port Office asked him not to enter but to anchor outside the channel and a pilot would be sent out at noon the following day to escort them in. Our friendly ship agreed in a tone of weary resignation and it was obviously going to delay him half a day. After the friendly ship anchored and we could view her from the side we saw how similar to her all the other lights were and that was when we realized they were all ships waiting to be given clearance to enter the port and had been told to wait outside.

There were seventeen ships all at anchor waiting

for daylight to enter the river to reach the port. This was a particularly treacherous estuary because it was full of sandbanks, and as is common with sandbanks, they moved over time.

It was five o'clock in the morning and we had been hove to since half past two. It was cloudy with no stars or moon visible. It was my watch. Francis had gone to bed at four and wanted to be woken at six. Out on the ocean doing a watch alone there is plenty of time to think. I watch the sea, the sky and any land and think about life. Not just one's own life but life generally.

Our brief time on this beautiful ball spinning in space is so precious to us yet we often make such a mess of it. The damage we humans do by our destruction of nature, polluting the land and sea, and especially by our over-breeding. We overfish, we force other creatures off land that we want to farm or build upon, we tear down forests, we are the invading weed on the planet. Stepping away from a town in to nature shows me how lucky I am to be alive and see the beauty.

I was tired and a little bit chilly. On my 4am to 6am watch I thought about being at home in Somerset and wondered what I was doing in South America instead of being tucked up in bed where in the mornings I could go outside and smell the flowers. At ten o'clock that morning I went to sleep for more than two consecutive hours at last! But first we had to get off a sandbank.

At seven a.m. I went to bed. Francis was steering us through Galheta Channel in the Bay of Paranaqua. I was woken at half eight when I felt the boat hit something firmly. Twice. Then a third time. A sandbank! I went on deck. Francis had put the engine into reverse but there was no change. We were stuck. In waters where there are sandbanks it is dangerous sailing, the sand shifting this way and that with the movement of the sea. Charts show, as far as they are able, where sandbanks are but the extent of each can change and they are generally invisible. Plainsong gave an enormous thud and shudder every ten seconds.

Chapter Fifteen

Francis inflated the dinghy and rowed out with an anchor to tow Plainsong off. The anchor rope stopped flowing smoothly. I moved from the helm to the bow and stood on the deck smoothing the rope as it left its bag. The shuddering continued making me rock about and almost fall. Once the anchor was in Plainsong began to lift then float. Slowly she turned and I steered her in the direction of the dredged channel. Francis came back to the boat, tied on the dinghy and as Plainsong moved through the water slowly he jumped aboard.

It had taken an hour to get free in light drizzle. We pulled up the anchor and re-anchored in deep water. I went back to bed hoping to get at least two hours sleep in a row It is my brother, Brian's birthday today. That night there was a huge thunder and lightening storm after midnight which lasted just over an hour. I got very little sleep.

Thursday, 6th August. Under way at six thirty five in the morning. Sails up at quarter past eight once there was a breeze. The breeze was good and gentle with the sun shining and we enjoyed a cup of tea and biscuits sitting in the cockpit sailing along a sunbeam.

We had come along Canal de Galheta (Channel of Galheta) and entered Baia de Paranaqua (Paranagua Bay) and anchored overnight near Ilha de Mel (Island of Honey). Ilha de Mel is in the state of Parana. Our next anchorage would be in the next state north, Sao Paulo, at Ilha de Bom Abrigo (Island of Good Shelter).

Galheta Channel is very narrow and is the shipping lane leading to the Port of Paranagua. On our way out we met a ship coming towards us from behind, then overtaking us. It was a container ship registered in Hamburg. It was clean and shiny and in good condition. The wash from it was no problem. Ten minutes later another large container ship came from the opposite direction. It had to pass between the first ship and us. It was registered in Bermuda and was not in immaculate condition. This ship created an enormous wash sending quick waves over our bow. Ugh! Too close for comfort but there was not much space in the shipping lane.

Yesterday on the Island of Honey we went by dinghy to a little cove for a walk. There was a small village in the cove where a dozen men were moving sacks of a dry cement like substance from the small pier to a building and then onto a barge. We walked across the narrow part of the island on a three feet wide sandy track that was formed between low houses. Ferns, moss and red hibiscus grew at the sides of the track. Out at sea we saw the blow and then tail fin of a whale. Riding back to the boat a dolphin swam along with us. In the bay that night we saw two fishing boats.

On Friday 7th we left the anchorage at four o'clock in the morning to go from Island of Good Shelter to Isle do Guarau. There was no wind so we motored all the way, anchoring at half past three in the afternoon. It was important to arrive in daylight because the chart showed many rocks and we didn't want to hit any.

The mountains and islands are spectacular. Tall, lush

green mountains and islands look as if they have spurted from the centre of the earth. In mid-afternoon I noticed a line of foam ahead and curving about one hundred yards to starboard. We checked the chart which showed this particular area clear of shoals and rocks. As we got closer we saw it was a tide line where the river Ribeira de Iguape met the ocean. In the foam were twigs and branches washed out into the sea. The mountains near our anchorage, Serra dos Itatins, soar to 4,500 feet. Isle do Guarau has many frigate birds flying around and palm trees sprout all over between the other trees.

Frigate birds are enormous yet fly gracefully with a tail rather like a swallow. The tail is long and forked, the beak long with a curved end and the body of the male of the type "magnificent" is dark except for a scarlet throat pouch which, when he is seeking a mate, swells to the size of a balloon. Its wing span can be eight feet which is almost as wide as the albatross which has a wing span of up to ten feet. I see many albatross and they too are fabulous although they don't have the splendid pouch and tail shape of the frigate bird. Tomorrow we will sail to Santos the biggest port in South America. It was founded in 1535 by Bras Cubas.

I've fallen in love. I've fallen in love with the night sky. When the night is clear the constellations are so magnificent that I stare facing the heavens in awe. A boat, especially a sailboat, is an excellent place from which to view the stars because you can be dozens, hundreds, or thousands of miles from land so there is little or no light pollution. There are places on land were visibility is good including spots designated as protected Dark Sky areas. There, in all their glory, are the wonderful, twinkling stars, as if someone had thrown handfuls of rubies and diamonds across a navy blue velvet cloak.

Some of the stars and constellations were named

hundreds of years ago, some of them thousands of years ago. A map of the heavens was drawn which enabled people like sailors and shepherds to have a rough idea of their direction of travel. It is mind-boggling to think that with binoculars or a telescope you can see what appears to be a bleary misty star and yet it is a another galaxy and there are thousands of them and some galaxies are bigger than ours. Mind-boggling.

Late the following afternoon having left Paranagua we anchored at what was shown on a maritime chart as an anchorage but merely turned out to be a relatively shallow place to anchor next to a tiny island about three miles from the rocky mainland. There was no cove or bay. It was like stopping on a highway. Frigate birds circled above. Francis wondered whether we should continue sailing on through the night to the next anchorage about ten hours away because this one looked so hopeless. I hoped we wouldn't have to keep sailing. Trying to be upbeat I said "Oh it probably won't be any worse than the places we have anchored in the Inner Hebrides in Scotland."

The anchorage proved to be useless. My hopes of a quiet night were wrong. The wind picked up and the Atlantic Ocean swell got bigger and we slopped about such that sleeping became difficult.

It is half two in the morning and I hadn't had a wink of sleep because of all the rocking and rolling at anchor. This was the poorest place to choose that I have ever stayed. The chart showed an anchorage on Isle do Guarau but really it was on the ocean highway with no protection. The island was tiny with no bay or cove. One just had to pick a spot with the least swell and wind and hope that the wind would not swing around to another direction – it did. We decided to continue sailing and were away again within half an hour.

So at half past two in the morning, under a dark, cloudy sky with the moon throwing a silvery brightness now and then across the water, we set sail for the port of Santos.

Francis had had some sleep and felt invigorated and glad to be on the move. It was a cloudy night with the full moon only occasionally appearing for a few seconds yet its brightness illuminated the night. For the first two hours the swell was eight feet high and it seemed scary to me as it rolled towards us in the darkness.

We arrived at Santos at half past one in the afternoon. The channel is narrow. Besides manoeuvring out of the way of three towering ships also entering Santos we had to weave around fifty small boats, like rowing boats with engines, that dotted the river. The area was smelly. There was a tall perimeter fence topped with five rows of barbed wire. There were flood lights every thirty feet and security lookout towers at the end of every section. There is a concrete walkway and a sloping section down to the boats. Under this concrete walkway is the marina wall with timber posts supporting the concrete. Under the walkway were yards of smelly, rotten garbage that has accumulated. I can't help thinking that cockroaches and rats would find it ideal and would crawl along our boat lines that tether us to shore.

Santos is a busy commercial city with the biggest port in South America. It started and grew by exporting sugar and coffee. The museum at Santos Football Club has a part dedicated to Pele, who played for the team for most of his career. Just north of it is the small town of Ubatuba some 200 miles south of Rio. It is in a large bay with idyllic beaches, sheltered from southern winds. Two mountains are visible from the sea, Corcovado Peak at 3,100 feet and Mount Corcovado at 3,700 feet.

Just inland is Minas Gerais. A State named after a company, General Mines. The company mined gold, diamonds and other precious stones from the 1700s. Exports from the state including electronics and cars go through Santos port.

This is a large State almost all of which is north and west of Rio. Belo Horizonte, its capital, is one of the largest cities in Brazil with hardly any buildings dated before the 1900s. State and National Parks all over Brazil, including here, are wonderful. Places to visit include a seminary (Santuario Do Caraca) that has tourist accommodation and a Zen Buddhist monastery near Linares which is open on Sundays and is in the neighbouring State of Espirito Santo.

Santos is a rather smelly harbour with a lot of debris yet is has the most beautiful yacht club facilities we have ever seen.

Santos Yacht Club (Iate Clube de Santos) is luxurious: Up to date, clean, with beautiful furniture and a fabulous marvellous marble shower and ladies room where delectable thick, white cotton towels are provided. In the bar there is a small locally made model of a wooden hull of a ship made in Liverpool. There is an attractive casual seating area and a gorgeous wood panelled restaurant adorned with good paintings and sketches, quite a few of which were of places in Britain. There are two water taxis to take sailors to their boat although we usually used our dinghy. It is good not to be alongside the quay where rats or insects could come aboard walking along the ropes tethering us to shore.

Our boat has been rodent and insect free because we have been scrupulous about what we bring on board. No large cardboard boxes are allowed because they could harbour cockroaches. We empty all the shopping into bags on the shore and put those into the dinghy taking the large cardboard boxes to the rubbish bins.

We dine at the Yacht Club on 10th August and I enjoy fillet steak with chips followed by and ice cream sundae. A treat after living on tinned food, a little veg, and the occasional fresh fish. I've been teaching myself the constellations when I am doing my night watches. The sky is so black that the stars twinkle with incredible and unusual brightness. The most spectacular constellation in the Southern Hemisphere is Scorpio. It is so huge it stretches right across the sky with three bright stars at one end then winding stars down towards its curved tail. Scorpio swivelled as the night wore on with the brilliant red supergiant star, Antares shining brightly.

Such marvellous stars, constellations, clusters and planets. The coal sack and the jewel box are in the milky way and look just like their names suggest. They are two of my favourites, so aptly named and so intriguing. Ptolomy described Scorpio in the second century. It had been known long before that because the Sumerians referred to it five thousand years ago calling it Gir Tab, meaning the Scorpion. It was also know to the Persians, the Egyptians and the Babylonians.

The myth is that Scorpio stung the mighty hunter Orion to death that is why they are placed on opposite sides of the heavens. Orion disappears as Scorpio rises. Almost all of Scorpio lies within the Milky Way and it shines with eleven stars all above the third magnitude including the amazing Antares. Antares, like Betelgeux, is a red supergiant and thought to be 700 times bigger than our sun and 10,000 times brighter. It is so large that it is unstable and pulsates with a changing brightness.

Sagittarius has a bow drawn with his arrow pointing to Antares, Scorpio's heart. Omega Centauri is actually a group of hundreds of thousands of stars. It is the finest example of a globular cluster visible to the naked eye.

Southern Cross is one of the smallest constellations. There are four main stars Alpha, Beta, Gamma and Delta. The Southern Cross, also known as Kappa Crucis or NGC 4755, has a prominent red supergiant that shines like a ruby. It lies at the edge of the Coal Sack, a large dark nebula.

One of my discoveries is the incredible tiny but

magnificent Jewel Box to the left of the Cross. The Jewel Box is an open cluster.

Centaurus, the centaur was half man half horse (some friends refer to people they don't like as Centaurs because they are half man and half horses ass). Chiron, the centaur said to be wise and a great teacher especially of hunting, healing and music but could not heal himself when accidentally hit by one of Heracles' poisoned arrows. (Hercules is the Roman form of the Greek name). Large and spectacular with feet in the Milky Way it has the third brightest star in the sky, Rigil Kent (Alpha), with only Sirius and Canopus brighter. Alpha is a double and is yellow. Beta (also called Agena) is blu'ish white.

After a few refreshing days at the Club and feeling squeaky clean from hot showers, we headed further north at 6.40 in the morning on 12th August towards Rio de Janeiro.

Half a dozen dolphins came and swam around the boat at half seven in the morning. The dolphins stayed with us for some time. Splish splosh, splish splosh, they jumped and dived around the boat and I was so happy to see them I sang:

Gorgeous dolphins
you make the day so bright.
When I see you,
the world is full of light.

We spent a night in a cove at As Ilhas. As Ilhas is a small charming island with deeply wooded hills and lovely small beaches. It was open from the south to the north west. There was no wind that night so we slept comfortably. Putting my head out of the companionway the following morning I could see the sea quite calm and no wind hitting me in the face. It was a calm day in which to motor towards San Sebastian channel.

We sailed passed Tock-Tock Island and on towards Isla Bela another two hours further. The sky was grey and low and the temperature warm. We had the sails up for an hour but the wind faded so it was back to motoring. It was late morning when we reached Isla Bella and as it was such a still day we decided to make miles while we were dry with no drizzle and with good visibility. The sun shone for two hours which is a record since sailing in Brazil. The brightness made shiny horseshoe shapes on the sea which glistened ahead of us. Corcovado mountain rose to 3,700 feet in the distance above the nearby hills. A dead penguin floated past our boat. It was sad to see and I hoped it died quickly of old age and didn't suffer. Sails went up again after lunch. We drifted softly and quietly into a lovely bay south of the town of Ubatuba and opposite Anchieta Island. I do adore the names of these places; Tock-tock, Ubatuba and Isle do Mel.

Fifty yachts were on moorings on one side of the bay so we went to the other, empty side. A few large, well maintained houses sat pleasantly on the waterfront and on the lush hillside. Behind the small golden beach, which was both clean and empty, rose Corcovado Peak, a different mountain that rises to 3,100 feet. That afternoon it was soon covered with low, grey cloud.

The saltwater intake in the galley is smelly. Francis is soon below the flooring of the boat, the lids are off the steps in the companionway, the huge wooden engine cover is next to the bunks and Francis is getting to the bottom of the saltwater inlet pipe.

We picked up several days worth of very full and informative copies of the New York Times in Santos and have been reading about Bill Clinton. I have been worrying about him for days. He has just made the stupid declaration that he did not have sexual relations with that woman, when it is obvious that he did. I wonder whether he can avoid making a hash of the remainder of his Presidency, which is likely if he continues to lie about his relationship.

Chapter Sixteen

Clinton is a great President. He really cares about changing things for the better for most of the American people, especially the poor. He has no prejudice. He has a terrific sense of humour, good charisma, and is highly intelligent. Clinton has tried to improve health care, education and tighten up the gun laws. Some organisations and businesses such as private health care, gun manufacturers and the tobacco industry do not like him.

Surely he realizes that the DNA evidence taken from the semen stain on Monica's dress is convincing evidence. Though why anyone would keep a dress in a cupboard with squirted, sticky semen on it makes one wonder. Clinton should admit he lied earlier because the Starr investigation is not primarily about whether Clinton had sex, it is about subverting the course of justice: he should just tell the truth.

If only people who lie about affairs realized the harm they do to their partner and to their colleagues. Hillary Clinton said, when rudely asked about their private life in an interview, that he was a hard dog to keep on the porch. Those staff members had to deal with the press and had asked Clinton whether he had an affair so that they could better deal with the fallout in the media about it, they were committed supporters and admired him yet they lost all respect and loyalty once they found he had lied to them, the people, along with his wife, who were closest to him. A good close relationship is something precious. It is like a beautiful vase. Once that is damaged and truth is lost it can never, ever be regained. The vase, though mended and stuck together again will always have that crack, that weak spot and will never again be that wonderful precious thing.

I'm enjoying reading The Third Chimpanze by Jared Diamond which I wanted to read after finishing The Selfish Gene several years ago. They come to mind now, both books, because I can't help but shake my head at the folly of men who suffer loss of office, loss of respect, often the loss of their marriage all brought down by short term sexual highs. A quick squirt and it screws up their life. For many men it looks as if their brains really are empty when their balls are full.

Did I gain any insight from the books? Yes, a tremendous amount. I wish I knew what I know now when I was younger and dating. The urge in the genes of men to procreate and leave as many replicas of themselves in as many women as possible was illuminating and that this urge really does, often overcome will-power in many, many males.

Men, so statistics and research tell us, are less discriminating about who they mate with because they invest less time and effort in the nurturing to maturity of those eggs they fertilize. Women are more choosey because they have to invest around eighteen years from the time their eggs are fertilized until their offspring are mature enough to fend for themselves and survive in the big wide world. Therefore, a woman's instinct is, normally, to only have enough children that she can nurture and care for whilst a man's instinct is simply to father or rather to breed and produce as many offspring as he can. Hence the spectacle he makes of himself screwing around his neighbourhood, whether that be the glitzy, rich places of Manhattan, Long Island, Aspen, London or Paris or other cities and villages around the world.

What is supposed to separate humans from other animals is our ability to analyse and act intelligently. Yet it is hard to see any analysis by a man goes on when a man propositions a woman or is propositioned by her. Hundreds of years ago the impulse to breed might have been understandable when life spans were short and the planet had enough resources for us all. Now the biggest danger to our planet is we humans. The urge and desire to breed is hardly now the intelligent choice. Humans are the third chimpanzee and our lack of forward planning shows. We are the weed of the earth, strangling and destroying much of what is around us. Breeding is now out of hand. Our population is so large that lions, tigers, elephants are just some of the animals whose homelands we take and destroy in order to make money or build or grow produce on what was their territory.

Saturday, 15th August. Under way at 6.40 am. Calm, so motored.

Yesterday we anchored in a bay part of Enseada do Flamengo. The village was not shown on our chart. We went ashore for a walk. The village may be called Perequeque Merim if we judge from the signs on the few shops. The day was warm and humid and I was overdressed, too hot and soon sticky. It had been a mistake to wear thick jeans, wellingtons and oilskins. This area has beautiful beaches and one has a waterfall nearby. Later we sail to Ubatuba.

Ubatuba is a small town on the mainland two hundred miles from Rio and forty miles south west of Parati. The bay is large and sheltered from the south which was the reason for choosing it. Much of the wind, when it blows, has been from the south. Two of the bays were sheltered to every wind but not south and one was sheltered mainly from the south. The wind piped up and for an hour we rushed along in winds of twenty five to thirty knots from the south. The first of the bays was the one with southerly protection so we made for that one and were glad to do so because the name intrigued us.

There is a pretty blue and white church, Igreja Exaltacao da Santa Cruz Matriz and some ruins to explore in the town. There is a turtle project and although the tanks are small the turtles are kept safe. When they can survive many are released.

Clear blue sky all day – amazing. Very warm so instead of layers of clothes and oilskins I'm wearing tee-shirt, shorts, a big hat and sunscreen. Haven't seen any ships for days. Francis has been smiling and happy because we had the sails up for hours in a good breeze.

In the late afternoon we arrive at Parati Mirim, a large inlet to the west of an irregularly shaped bay making it very protected. Tropical coastal rainforest covers the hills which rise steeply from the sea. Bits of sandy beach lie here and there under the hills. Francis is finding the heat unpleasant after six months in the roaring gales of southern Chile and Argentina. He put up the bimini over the cockpit to give us protection from the strong, hot sun.

Tonight we have a radio schedule call with Robi and Lyn on the boat "Soolaimon". We connect on single side band radio on a pre-arranged frequency and time. We talk every few days unless they or us are doing an offshore passage when we try to talk each night. They are fun, lighthearted and practical and from New Zealand. Francis met them at a yacht marina in Mar del Plata, Argentina.

Our walk ashore was on a track through the rainforest near a clear, meandering river. We passed a couple of swaying bridges. Each was ten feet over the river and about a quarter of a mile apart. They were made of thick rope and wood which swayed when walked upon. Pink hibiscus grew along fences near the few village houses. There was a small Indian reservation with small houses constructed of wooden walls and dry grass roofs. There was a large amount of litter. I wonder if they have rubbish collection here? Woven baskets of grass edged in pink or purple ribbon hung up for sale on a low rail near the track. Three dark haired, dark eyed children ran towards us shouting words we couldn't understand but which seemed to be a version for foreigner. Corn and sugar cane grew in small patches, papaya and banana trees were abundant.

After only 4 miles of a round trip walk we stopped to eat at a stall on the beach before untying the dinghy and rowing back to the boat. We ordered fish and chips and the fish was cut vertically and fried still whole with its bones and eyes intact.

Tuesday, 18th August. Isle de Cotia. This is a small anchorage, protected on all sides by hills and mountains. Going ashore we found a thirty foot wide sandy trail through the narrowest part of the island. It looked out across a little boulder-strewn cove. Large turquoise butterflies drifted and fluttered their three inch wings between the small trees as the pale blue sea gently lapped the shore.

That evening we were going over to Robbie and Lyn's boat also in this anchorage to share supper. I prepared the vegetables on our boat and intended to cook them and take them over at our meeting time. The vegetables and sauce just needed 3 minutes in the pressure cooker. Uh-uh - no gas. The only time we had arranged to share the cooking and I can't cook anything! It was quarter to six and we were due at their's at six. Francis changed the gas bottle. It was six o'clock. We tried the gas. It didn't work. We rowed over to Robbie and Lyn's and explained what happened and they put our pot on their gas and all was well. They had made an egg and tomato flan. The talk was of keeping the drinking water tanks clean, what food keeps best for meals when one cannot buy supplies for weeks at a time and how one has to be adaptable for all the things that go wrong, like the freezer packing up so there is nothing but tinned food to eat for weeks.

Wednesday, 19th August. Vera, John and Raul came for coffee at nine in the morning. They are fashionable, good looking and full of enthusiasm about life. They are Brazilian, live in Sao Paulo and are enjoying a holiday here on Vera and John's sailboat. They all spoke good English and as our Portuguese was very limited we kept to English. Some of the chat was about the Football world cup and the Brazil v France game which Brazil lost. They thought the team were simply exhausted. Ronaldo has good deals with his team and with Nike which make him a multi-millionaire. The mobile telecommunications business is booming. One of the strange things is that in third world or lower income countries to get a land line installed can take several years. The system is slow to meet the needs of the population and expensive. What has happened is that the society has jumped the technology for land lines and jumped straight into mobiles – Immediately available, portable, and low cost. There is talk that an AT&T deal with BT will help business to be more efficient and profitable. Vera, John and Raul wanted to meet up again and I was keen because they were so interesting. They recommended a bird book by Fritz Foster to me. Francis was vague and didn't make any firm plans because he wanted to be free of meeting anyone other than Robbie and Lyn.

Between Ubatuba and Rio is one of the prettiest towns anywhere. This is Parati. Its narrow cobbled streets allow few vehicles. There are cheerfully painted boats and a high tide that rushes up the streets gurgling below the pavements. It has little beautiful shops and large status being a UNESCO World Heritage site. Once a port to ship the gold from Minas Gerais it now has some fishing and farming and much tourism.

We spent a week around the eighteenth century Portuguese colonial town. It is about 4 hours driving northeast of Sao Paulo and about 3 hours southwest of Rio. It has streets paved with large cobbles and some of the streets flood up to six inches at high tide taking all the small debris out to sea. The windows and door frames of the white washed houses are often painted turquoise and many windows have wooden shutters opened against the wall. The Chapel of St Rita is a white washed building on the small seafront.

For those who don't like small and pretty places and prefer modern cities then Sao Paulo might be just the place. It is made for those doing business or who like the stark, modern tall buildings. It does have several good museums and a rather interesting museum with a research institute, the Butantan Institute. Here horrible looking insects and other crawlies can be seen behind glass. To my horror there is a bird-eating spider the size of a football. It does not often eat birds more commonly filling itself with lizards or mice. This type of tarantula is the largest spider there is.

For something less scary there is the Museum of Art with well laid out galleries with art from 1500s Italian through Dutch, French, English and Brazilian to the 1900s. For more Brazilian art see the Pinacoteca, especially the sister gallery Estacao Pinacoteca with its political history display on the ground floor.

The Government building of Palacio Capanema was built in 1936. It was designed by Le Corbusier and he put together the outstanding modernist team of Lucio Costa, Roberto Marx and Oscar Niemeyer. This team built the new capital Brasilia though it led to huge government debt.

Visit the fabulous Football Museum in the Pacaembu Stadium which opened in 2008 and that has interesting information. Having the museum in Rio might have brought it more foreign visitors and all those young amateur players on the beaches would learn more about their heroes. Perhaps in future they might have a sister museum in Rio. Surprising to think an Englishman, Charles Miller, brought the sport to the country.

Gorgeous Parati was busy in the seventeen hundreds when it was used to ship out valuable minerals, especially gold, from the State of Minas Gerias (General Mines) and then coffee and sugar. The town flag has on it a stalk of sugar cane and a branch of a coffee tree. Until the 1970s there was no paved road so getting to it was difficult. Now it takes in flocks of fashionable tourists and even has a literary festival. One of the prettiest and trendiest places in Brazil, it has access to some of the small nearby islands for walking or snorkelling.

20th August, Robbie's birthday. Lyn and Robbie came over to our boat for drinks and we drank small drams of Scottish Whisky. Much of our chat was about architecture in various parts of the world and the keystones supporting arches. We imagined how dangerous it used to be for the workers fifty to a hundred years ago when less attention was paid to worker safety. In those days there was no warning about entering a hard hat area. Francis said "Yes, in those days you were entering a hard luck area!"

As we were leaving I said I wouldn't be up at dawn the next day. Francis said there was a joke that Ronald Reagan when campaigning never got his team to start before the crack of noon. Ronald Reagan was Governor of California before becoming President and lived in Pacific Palisades and Santa Barbara. Reagan was quick witted and friendly with charisma. He also shared some of the unfortunate hardline policies of Margaret Thatcher. He had an office in the same building where I worked in Avenue of the Stars in Century City, Los Angeles.

The next day we moved to another cove in Parati Bay. It was narrow and we were towing our dinghy. As we reversed to get ready to do the anchor the engine groaned then silence. The dinghy rope had got tangled around the propellor. Six white herons glanced over to us from nearby boulders. Donning goggles, snorkel and blue flippers, Francis lowered himself into the warm water. The rope was tightly wound and wouldn't come free. I made a rope sling over the side of the boat for Francis to hold on to when he wanted to take a breath.

Francis asked for a vegetable knife. A few minutes after ducking into the water his head appeared, then his arms and he handed me the kitchen knife minus the blade. He asked for the bread knife – the only other very sharp knife on board. This time it worked. He threw pieces of rope onto the deck and the bread knife remained intact. We had three attempts at anchoring but couldn't get the anchor to dig in. We motored two minutes away and tried again and this time it was successful.

Under low grey clouds we set off the next morning motoring the three miles back to Parati. The rev counter and temperature gauge have stopped working. This may have happened when the rope became entangled in the propeller. The dinghy has sprung a leak, probably caused by rubbing against barnacles at a pontoon when we first came to Parati. The leak was soon mended with waterproof tape. Low clouds drift across the valleys and hide the mountains. The bay is calm with a silver shimmer meandering across it. Fish sparkling in the light are jumping, tern are calling and small, brightly painted fishing boats are heading for the town wharf.

We are picking up Didi and Edward and their two children Alexander aged ten and Henrietta aged four from Parati and taking them sailing with us for a couple of days. They are English. They used to live in Hampshire and the Isle of Wight. Now they live in Sao Paulo, the biggest city in South America, with 12 million people. Edward's work brought him and his family here eighteen months ago and they are thrilled with the variety of landscapes and the very different lifestyle.

There is much kissing of cheeks and shrieks of hello as we greet each other on the pontoon. We load their duffel bags into the dinghy and everyone squeezes in. We are off on our weekend adventure. We all sit around the cockpit with our hot, fragrant and steamy chicken casserole supper in dishes and eat eagerly as darkness falls.

Edward has made us "caipirinhas" a Brazilian drink made with sugar cane alcohol called Cachaca to which is added limao – a cross between a lemon and a lime. Normally limes are used. The lime or limao is mashed with the sugar and then the Cachaca is poured on top and ice added if wanted. Later feeling full and content we went below deck.

Bedtime was rather a scrum. Didi and Edward had the double bunk. Alexander and Henrietta had the top bunks, I had a bottom bunk and Francis slept outside folded up on the port side cockpit seat. Or he did until one o'clock in the morning when it rained heavily. Then he moved inside and slept folded up in the small seat at the chart table, head lolling by the extra compass and feet over the engine cover towards the cooker. I offered to swop places with him but he insisted that he was happy where he was. He wanted our guests to be comfortable and didn't mind the short term discomfort. Over the next two days we slowly sail to two anchorages on the southern side of the bay a few miles away from the town. We all share pulling on the lines, shaking out the sails, and taking the helm and making sandwiches. On Sunday morning we sail back to the town under a clear sky. On the way we eat a sandwich and fruit lunch sitting on the deck in the sunshine. Didi and Edward and the children are driving back home to Sao Paulo. The boat seems dull and quiet once they have gone.

We leave Parati for Ilha Grande at 7 a.m. on a warm Monday morning under blue sky. The mountains all around are dark in the weak morning light. The heat grew as the day went on. There were markers for a measured mile so we motored a mile each way and checked the compass and the GPS. Ilha Grande Bay is a wide area which has all these lovely places of Parati Mirim, and Parati and the Bay of Stars. Ilha Grande is a hilly car free island with beaches, waterfalls and rain forest. Architecturally stunning with outdoor cafes and pleasant galleries. It was once a leper colony and then a high security prison. Ilha Grande is part of Angra dos Reis (Bay of the Kings). There are over two hundred small islands in this area. The water may be a little warmer than the sea further away because it gets the heated run off from the local nuclear power station. It is a rare part of the world where tropical, sub-tropical and temperate waters meet. The island has howler monkeys, sloths and parrots.

Chapter Seventeen

It was magical entering the Bay of Stars, the Enseada da Estrella, and then over to a small cove on the north east side of the bay on Isla Grande called Sack of the Sky or Cove of the Sky, Saco do Ceu. The Bay of Stars has many places to anchor though in some winds a swell can roll in. The Sack of the Sky cove is wonderfully protected from swell and wind with high, wooded hills all around. Our anchorage looks across to a narrow sandy beach on the far side of the main bay while being enfolded by steep rainforest. The many birds call all day though especially in the early morning and early evening. Insects are noisy most noticeably in the quiet of the night when the air is filled with a high pitched buzzing and whirring. The sound is similar to that sometimes heard emanating from electricity wires that stretch from pole to wooden pole.

We decided to go for a walk on the other side of the bay. We took the dinghy and surfed in on it as the waves were strong and flung us, hearts pounding, onto the beach. We jumped quickly from the dinghy before it could be pulled back by the sea, and grabbed the rope at the front to pull it up the beach and tie to a rock. We passed a grand entrance to a private house. A wooden platform stretched across the narrow section of beach from garden to sea. There was a guard house near a gateway. There was a model, larger than life, of an astronaut in the garden.

Numbers were painted on large boulders on the beach from one to eleven. A satellite dish sat on some of them. The sand was grainy under foot the colour of warm gold; rock pools of clear water trickled over star fish and all around was the dense foliage of jungle.

Vera and John had recommended a walk to take us to a delightful viewpoint which we did the next day. I cover up well because I don't want to be bitten by insects. My pale trousers are tucked into socks and the ground is dry so my tennis shoes won't get muddy. I've put on a long sleeved shirt and put sunscreen and insect repellent on my exposed skin. As always when the sun shines, I wear a sunhat. Putting the dinghy against the bright yellow fenders of the pontoon belonging to a small café we clambered on to dry land. At the café we admire Nina the beautiful long haired Siamese cat and look at the painted plates for sale. The owner of the café selected two walking sticks to help us on our climb. It would take only just over ten minutes to reach the top but it was a hard walk. The hillside was steep with carved, rough hewn steps most of the way. Bamboo neatly edged the steps. A ginger and white shorthaired cat came along with us as we picked our way up the zigzag slope through bamboo groves. Trees and ferns I couldn't recognize surrounded us. At the top two ladders attached to a huge boulder lead to a place to sit and observe the view over the tranquil bay. One of the ladders is rather old bits of bamboo tied together. The other, perhaps only a year old, is neatly cut, machine straight wood. Down below are tiny looking motor boats crossing the bay. Small houses like matchboxes sit near the edge of the aquamarine water. Two shallow patches show up in the sunlight, reaching out from rocks near the shore.

Friday, 28th August. Sail to the Bay of Palms and Mangrove Beach (Enseada das Palmas and Praia dos Mangues).

I've got a cold or stomach bug and am feeling well below par. I feel achey all over and unwell.

Praia dos Mangues is protected and quiet. Most of the island is an ecological reserve. Walked a short distance across a narrow, low part of the island to the roaring ocean swell on the other at Praia de Lopes Mendes. This beach is long with creamy, soft, flour like fine sand.

The next day Francis went off for a trek to the small fishing village of Abraao. This has a protected and pretty bay which was one and a quarter hours each way over the hills, through rainforest where he saw small monkeys jumping from tree to tree.

It rained heavily all the next day. We stayed on board and I read books still feeling unwell.

Monday. Sailed towards Rio!

Left at four o'clock in the morning when it was still dark. Motored. Went below to sleep at seven o'clock but didn't sleep because the sea was lumpy.

Rio was to be our next big port of call.

Sailing up the coast to Rio de Janeiro, (The Bay or River of January founded by Amerigo Vespucci in January, 1502) we entered the magical sight of mountains and hills that look as if they spurted from the sea and have been frozen in position. Forests of National and City parks fill the hillsides. The long sandy beaches of Ipanema, then Copacabana lead us to Sugar Loaf Mountain with Mount Pico on the other side of Guanabara Bay. It is astonishingly beautiful.

Looking towards Guanabara Bay the sails full, the boat skimming the water, I was dazzled by the beauty. Francis and I jabbered excitedly to each other pointing out soaring, narrow mountains rising from the sun dappled sea, islands, islets, golden beaches, dark container ships coming and going, small motor boats whizzing around enjoying the day with Corcovado mountain and Sugar Loaf the welcoming features of the face of Rio.

We entered Rio de Janeiro, Guanabara Bay at four o'clock in the afternoon after sailing all day. It was a truly magnificent sight. Wonderful mountains, islands, islets, skyscrapers, ships, small boats and beaches all dazzled in the sunlight. Our friends on Sooliamon were sailing just an hour ahead of us and led the way towards The Naval Yacht Club, our destination. It is a large bay and our boats are relatively slow. Darkness fell and we still had an hour of sailing to go. We slowed our speed and gently felt our way into the bay. It was difficult to tell where the marina was so we anchored near the shore and decided to go into the yacht club at Niteroi the following morning.

In Rio, we spent our first night anchored between three distant points: Sugar Loaf Mountain, Corcovado Mountain with its Christ statue, and third the modern day landmark - McDonalds food sign. The splendor of the bay sparkled in the morning sun when we awoke the next day. Sugar loaf and Corcovado mountains were easy to pick out. We moved to a better anchorage in Niteroi opposite Rio. It is a pleasant neighbourhood and quieter than Rio and only a short bus journey, just over eight miles away. It was once, for a short while, the capital of the State of Rio de Janeiro when the City of Rio was a separate entity. Then the City and the State merged and Niteroi passed the baton on to Rio allowing Niteroi to settle into its stable lifestyle. It is residential rather than touristy, although Oscar Neimayer's Museum of Contemporary Art is in Niteroi. The sea in the Bay is dangerous and in Niteroi it has a strong undertow. Its name means "hidden waters".

Rio is one of the most spectacular cities in the world. Mounds and rounded rocks and hillocks jut out of the sea and one can imagine the hot lava spurting from the earth and then being caught and frozen in motion leaving us with this wonderful scene.

It is winter there so the tourist beaches were almost empty but by dusk the beaches used by locals are full of young people, males and females, playing football, fishing or flying kites.

We took a few days to recover, sleep, and clean the boat. After that was done we went into Rio with Lyn and Robbie on the bus and ferry. Niteroi is across the other side of the bay to Rio so we have a good view of the city. There are charming nineteenth century cobbled streets with two storey houses which have brightly painted doors and window frames. Pretty wrought iron balconies and wrought iron street lamps hang centrally across the street from iron archways. There are some historic houses to see from the exterior and good parks.

A medium sized supermarket is rather average. It does not have the variety found in the USA or Papeete. An engine repair man is trying to find out why the rev counter on Plainsong is not working. The day is very hot though there are a few high cirrus clouds so I wonder if a cold front is moving in?

Chapter Eighteen

Rio has a happy, party atmosphere. It is where the Samba and the Bossa Nova started, where the song "The Girl from Ipanema" was written and where there are four large, well-supported football clubs : Flamengo; Vasco; Fluminense and Botafogo and the Maracana Stadium and where they remember with pride the Formula One racing champion, Aryton Senna. I've enjoyed several of Paulo Coelho's's books which are available all around the world. Other successful writers are Jorge Amado and Carmen Oliveira.

Like many big cities there are areas where crime is more prevalent. Sensible precautions such as not wearing expensive watches and jewellery and dressing casually as well as keeping an eye out for people taking a particular interest in you will all help you enjoy your time here.

It has had a difficult political history over the past 60 years especially during the 80s and 90s when it had soaring inflation of between 300 and 1,000%. The three previous Presidents have tried to deal with education and inflation. However, during the exuberance of being awarded responsibility for hosting the 2014 World Cup some questionable decisions were made. This time, as is often the case, the people were right to question some of the spending such as the money spent on the 42,000 seat stadium in the heat of Manus which previously held 36,000 spectactors and was normally the venue for a 4th division club.

Some twelve cities delayed or dropped plans for projects related to the World Cup. In contrast to the money spent in the areas where the average poorer person lives, remembering these are the areas many players grew up, it showed a lack of respect for those people.

We sat on beautiful Copacabana with its fine, silky soft sand; its heyday gone it is bordered by noisy cars and low price shops. Go along to Ipanema and Leblon where the young and wealthy enjoy sunbathing and watching beach life. Ipanema means dangerous waters in Brazilian Indian language and the sea does have large waves and a strong undertow. Everyone seems to wear flipflops. They are easy to wear and your feet breathe. The dress code is casual and the bikinis the tiniest I have seen. The women on the beaches must be the most beautiful and curvaceous in the world. I mention this to a male Rio resident, Alex, who says they all love to look good and some of them have a little surgical help then he winks at me and smiles. I really don't know why they bother to have surgery. They are an attractive people with a great country. "The fruit in your country is delicious," I say. "Yes, it is good," he replies. "When I went to school we would often pick a small mango to eat on the way." We look at people playing volleyball on the beach. "Is it difficult to learn?" I ask. "No," he replies. "It is a piece of cake. We say it is papaya with sugar."

Rio is stuffed with interesting places to visit including Christ the Redeemer Statue, or as they call it in Brazil, Cristo Redentor, on top of Corcovado mountain. The statue was designed by Frenchman Paul Landowski and built of soapstone by two engineers Heitor da Silva Costa and Albert

Caquot. The face was scuptored by Romanian Gheorghe Leonida. It has magnificent views on a clear day. By night it is brightly lit. It is advisable to go only in the day and on a clear one. The best way is by tram, which run frequently. I took a tram ride to the top with a driver and guide, Carlos while the others dealt with boat paperwork. Below like little dinky buildings lay the magnificent city with tiny ribbons of roads. The lagoon sparkled in the sun. Behind it the pale playgrounds of Ipanema and Copacabana beaches snuggled up to the sea.

Dream like mounds lay in the sea formed from the molten centre of our planet looking like sleeping elephants, though only for a brief time because soon a thick mist like a heavy grey blanket blew in from the sea and obscured everything, the apparent elephants, the beaches and even the one hundred and twenty five foot statue. If I had arrived ten minutes later I would have missed this stunning sight.

This statue is a favourite for many. Yet it seemed smooth, emotionless and lifeless, without the beauty of the Statue of Liberty done by another French sculptor, or the vigor of Michelangelo's work or the message conveyed by Rodin's The kiss. Perhaps the arms were too straight? I don't know why it didn't appeal to me. Sugar Loaf hill gets its name some say from the tin used as a mold for sugar or from a native words for an isolated hill. Both suit it. Sugar Loaf has a high cable car giving distant views that are so fabulous that the cable car was used in the Bond film "Moonraker".

In the afternoon I walked along the edge of the waves on Copacabana beach. Little soft flurries of sunlit water between my toes brought reminders of my home beaches. In my mind, just for a few moments, I was walking on them from Malibu to Santa Monica. Memories tugged at my heart. Deep longing suddenly filled me for my friends there, for that home in Los Angeles with its brilliant blue sea, its brown pelicans, howling coyotes, long eared owls, silk floss trees and the coral and the jacarada trees. Memories, so many happy memories, a decade of enchantment and paradise, of good, happy, friends sharing times, sharing food, strolling, chatting, sitting looking out into the Pacific came back to me. The hard part was that I had begun another chapter in the book of life and knew that I would probably never go back there.

That evening Francis and I look at the charts once again for the sail up to Salvador I am confirmed in my view that I want to go by bus for that part of the journey. The tides can be strong, the wind blustery and there are few places to anchor. Francis finds a local sailor to do that part of the trip up to Salvador and I will meet him there. The next day we go into Rio at lunch time by bus and ferry to book tickets and hotel in Salvador. We have to wait in travel agency queue for forty five minutes to get bus ticket to Salvador, then wait, sitting down this time, a further hour to book the hotel. It is all done by quarter past five. The day has gone. There is no time to go to a Brazilian football match or catch up on email in a computer shop. We have a cup of coffee and catch the bus back.

The bus was very crowded because it was rush hour. I stayed standing close to the entrance of the bus so that we could exit when we saw where we were. A large man in a blue denim shirt and jeans got on and asked me to move down. I shook my head and made space for him to pass indicating with my arm to go along into the bus. There were only overhead straps further down the bus which I could not reach. Here I could hold the pole. I said in Portuguese that he should go on. He moved as if to push past me but stopped right next to me. He was six foot tall and overweight. He pushed me hard against two other people and against the post next to me. My sunglasses dangling on a string broke. It was hard to breathe as the post dug into my chest. He stood behind me and pressed harder and harder. My eyes began to water with the pain and I felt suffocated. Then after just a few seconds he moved away. I felt as if I was an orange that had been squeezed dry. Other passengers look at me with sympathy but no-one did anything. A nice kind man motioned to me to move a few feet where space had opened up. We get back to the boat at half past seven.

The next day we go back to Rio to check email in a computer shop. Surprise! I got a funny email that made me laugh from my sister, Pauline. It is an odd thing this sailing. You live quite alone or almost alone, with little contact with any friends or family so the letters and messages that you do get mean a lot. Francis had an email from a friend, Johnny, who crewed with him when they sailed together on Plainsong around Cape Horn. I'd been in Ushuaia but Cape Horn was not my dream. Not only was it not my dream it would be a nightmare so I didn't do that leg. In the event the sea was flat calm when they did it so they did it again a week later when a roaring gale blew through and they thought that was great fun. Johnny enjoyed it so much he had a boat built to do a similar long distance journey around parts of the world that Francis had done.

Robbie and Lyn were complaining with Francis joining in too about a particularly noisy dog that keeps us all awake or wakes us from a deep sleep with its insistent loud barking all night. Lyn said "Someone should put something in its ear." "Yeah," said Robbie "a piece of lead".

A week passed as we explored, walked, talked and did boats jobs. The city has numerous festivals including the carnival, the New Year and Easter parades and parties, Indians Day in April, Day of St. George, Independence Day, Gay Pride Day and the marathon. The summer is December to March and the low season is May to September though the

Horses grazing on the sand

wettest can be October to February.

There are good galleries, museums and the fascinating Botanical Garden founded in 1808. There is an Indian Museum in Botafogo with the history of the native indigenous people and a mineral and jewels museum in the headquarters of the jewellers, H. Stern in Ipanema.

Along Rio's creamy beaches and the beaches of Niteroi, across the bay, football is being played. Tiny four year olds, the leggy teens, the strong 20 and 30 year olds right up to groups in their 60s and 70s are playing barefoot in the soft sand. You can see the joy in their faces and on mine and other passersby as we watch them in wonder at the beauty of their balletic and athletic movements. This sense of joy is visible and is a powerful and important ingredient not only in sport but also in life.

In many clubs around the world this sense of fun has gone, replaced by a sense of entitlement to high fees by players and high returns for sponsors and owners. Play has got dirtier. Some players intentionally or recklessly causing injury to other players with their aggressive tackles using arms and legs and being so in the face the other player barely has space to breathe. Any day now someone may set up another football organisation with clean play and showing all this wonderful balletic talent! Uruguay hosted the first World Cup and was the first winner. Italy and Germany have each won 4 times. Brazil 5 times with the admirable performance of winning 70 of 104 matches.

Young people play futebol, futsal (an indoor 5 aside game played quickly with flair) and beach football. In Rio football is a beautiful game. Here on the soft sand of Rio budding players enjoy the game and are being nurtured not just to play but to enjoy.

On a Monday evening Francis and I went to the bar at the yacht club. A slim, trendy man in his late twenties bought us a drink. He was with two friends and I wasn't sure they were trustworthy. I didn't want a drink from strangers. Francis encouraged me to accept so I did. Awful. I had a caipirinha that didn't taste of any caipirinha I'd had before. It was terribly strong and I didn't like it. "It's just a new drink, darling. There's nothing wrong with it. Drink up," Francis said when I said it tasted awful. My vision became blurred. Half an hour later I went to shower at the Yacht Club a minute walk away and lurched and swayed all the way there. The floor and ceiling seemed to change places, the walls seemed to do the twist. It was difficult to stand up.

It was the quickest shower I ever took. I couldn't stand. I let the water wash the shampoo from my hair and soap from my body as I sat on the floor. After showering I met up with Francis at the bar because we had arranged to do that and because I knew my mind was fuddled and I wouldn't easily find my way back to the boat. We and the three men went back to the boat where I lay on my bunk and groaned. Walking back I leaned on Francis because I could hardly walk. He laughed. "Darling, I've never seen you like this. It's the first time you've been drunk. How exciting!"

"No, it isn't. It's horrible."

It seemed to me that the drink was spiked. Down in the cabin while the men were on deck I told Francis, with slow, slurred speech what I thought. My bodies reaction was so severe I knew it wasn't simply alcohol. I told him quietly and with difficulty because my mouth wouldn't form the words, it was as if I had lost the power to control any part of my body, that he had to be careful; that it could have been a set up and that the men would steal from the boat. Francis laughed and said "It is just probably because you haven't eaten much all day. The guys are fine."

"They are strangers," I said.

"It's okay. They are okay. Just have a nice sleep and you'll feel fine later." He smiled then joined the three men on deck where they laughed and chatted for three hours and I slept deeply, very deeply. It was the first time in my life I'd been drunk and it would be the last. It is hard to know why anyone would think that drinking too much and spending way too much money on drink to feel like this is anything other than putting your brain in hell.

Years later I found that men drugging women is not uncommon. In Brazil several types of drugs are used to rape or rob women, the most common is known as Goodnight Cinderella. Goodnight Cinderella renders a woman unconscious or in a walking blackout. This is what I believe spiked my drink.

Goodnight Cinderella is sometimes colourless and is usually bought at a bar by a new friend. Don't accept a drink from a stranger unless you see the drink poured and it doesn't leave your sight. The symptoms begin with drowsiness, slurring of speech and general muscular grogginess which can be mistaken for drunkenness. Drug cocktails such as ketamine-flunifrazepam and GHB – Gamma hydroxybutyrate the ingredients of Goodnight Cinderella can be deadly. If a person thinks they have been given it then they should be tested for it within 6 hours or urine tested within 12 hours because these leave the system quite quickly. Project GHB in Arizona gives information about these drugs and the dangers and has an excellent article called "Wake up Cinderella" on their website.

Two days later Francis and I took a bus up to Fort Sao Luis which is on a nearby hilltop. It is very steep to reach the summit. On the top were disused cannon. It is one of the oldest still in use Military installations in the Americas. It is not open every day and there is a small charge or donation. The views over Niteroi, Sugar Loaf and Rio were stunning. Beautiful white trumpet shaped flowers with a single yellow stamen grew on the hillside. They had six petals which were three inches long and two inches wide. There was no noticeable fragrance. They grew in clumps with leaves like long grass. As we walked about we were watched by two intelligent looking black vultures. The vultures sat on the top railing above the surrounding wall, their heads smooth like black leather.

Three days later we visited the fascinating and beautiful Botanic Garden over near Copacabana. Palm trees make me think of sunny skies and I enjoy seeing the different types. It seemed to me in my ignorance that there might be about twenty types of palm tree. It was a surprise to discover that this garden has 6,000 species of plants including 900 varieties of palm trees. It was a joy to see so many beautiful palms including the King Palm, and the Bamboo palm also called Golden Cane palm which originally came from Madagascar. I walked amongst the 137 hectares of Bamboo palms from Madagascar, the tall Imperial palms from Guyana and feathery bamboo arching over paths. There are Pau Brazil trees (caesalpinia echinata) used for red dye and from which the country gets its name; Pau meaning wood and brasil meaning red and ember like.

Sailors, from 1500 onwards, called the country the land of the red dye tree, or the Land of Brasil. They are hardwood with delightful fragrant yellow flowers. It has an orange – red heartwood which can give a high shine. It is highly durable and dense yet workable. Its importance for bows for stringed instruments was recognised around the world. No other wood has the acoustic and workable qualities that make it desirable for bows for violas, violins and cellos. Unfortunately it is now on the endangered list because of over harvesting so that there is very little left of this wood. The Global Trees Campaign has worked with organisations to stop the extinction of this plant. It has worked with Lineas Reserve to re-introduce it there and the Rio Botanical Garden and the Margaret Mee Foundation of Cambridge, England.

There are Mango trees and ginseng brasilero. Then I saw the mind boggling Victoria water lilies which grow in shallow water and come from the native shallow water of the Amazon. The Victoria lily pad grows to nine feet in diameter on a stalk which can be as long as twenty six feet. They are amazing. They open white on their first night of opening and open pink on their second night. They are fragile if something hard and thin lands on it but if the weight is displaced across the whole pad it remains intact.

Fantastic weird orchids of pink, yellow and brown were enticing bees to pollinate them. An orchid house with interesting information about the difficulty of pollination with the seeds blown on the wind not containing many nutrients so they have to obtain them from nearby fungus. Some orchids are like vines so they cling to a tree or other plant yet do not take nutrients from the support plant.

The word "orchid" was first used by Theophrastus in 300 BC in the time of Aristotle. It meant testicles because that is what the root resembles. Witches are said to use the roots for magic potions, fresh for love and dry for passion. Orchids like light but not direct strong sunlight especially when in flower. They also like to be free draining, not to sit in water and quite dry before being watered.

It is almost time to make preparations to leave for the town of Salvador in Bahia State in the North. Francis had not been to the top of Corcovado and I encourage him to see the view. It is a clear day and the air is sweet when we set off. Corcovado means hunchback. The mountain is rounded at the top. From the top we see a dozen ships awaiting their turn to enter the docks. Our anchorage at Charitas in Niteroi is hidden by a hillside. Our bay is clearly protected from all directions. The view down one side is of the industrial sector while the other is of Ipanema and Copacabana. Francis is pleased by the view of the city and bay.

Carlos and his wife came along to the boat at three o'clock to share mugs of tea and slices of cake with us. They were a lovely couple and knowing them even a little added to our enjoyment of Rio.

Brazil is an enthralling place. It is a beautiful country with helpful, hospitable people. Though there is street crime you can generally avoid it if you keep your wits about you. You must keep in mind that our western way of dress might look opulent and cause envy or a wish to steal from us. Therefore it is sensible to dress down when walking about. Don't wear jewellery other than a wedding ring if married and only wear a simple cheap watch and don't carry anything other than a cheap bag.

In places the sea is much like the sea in some parts of Europe, dirty, brown and plastic bottles float on the water and line some of the shore. The Atlantic seems a very dirty ocean compared to the parts of the Pacific. The California coastline is mostly clean because the inhabitants follow the strictly enforced laws, with heavy fines, to not toss rubbish into the sea and not emptying ship and boat lavatories near the shore but instead have holding containers on board then pump out at various stations on the shore. The Polynesian islands too have problems with tourism that brings in plastic which the island people cannot then get rid of. Plastic is major problem everywhere.

Now, after a month in Rio it is time to go north, me by bus and Francis by boat to the State of Bahia.

Packed up some stuff: clothes, books and sunhat to take with me by bus to Salvador. Francis had one crew member to join him for that leg of the cruise that I didn't want to do. I'd stay in a hotel in Salvador for a few days until Plainsong arrived. I go to a phone cabin to call my family. My father is in hospital having a bladder and prostate operation and should be home a week after it. Mum said he hates being in hospital, that it is very boring with the shared television only tuned to soap operas and he never gets to see documentaries and in depth news programmes.

Chapter Nineteen

Got up the next day at six o'clock and caught the bus to Salvador at seven. Only about fifteen passengers. More get on at Petropolis. Travelled very high up on steep, narrow, mountain roads. Gorgeous valleys everywhere. After four hours the landscape changed to rolling countryside with cattle grazing. Saw two plump buffalo run down a hill away from two thin farmers who had been holding on to them to mow.

Spent an uncomfortable night scrunched up on two seats. Got a crick in my neck and backache. At half past four in the morning I decided to give up trying to sleep. I told myself that soon I would be in my hotel and could sleep there. Dawn was clear. The pale light crept up over the mountains to the east. The hills looked grey and stretched into the distance. We didn't pass towns, just isolated single small, single storey houses every few miles with tile roofs and with fences a few yards from the house.

At half ten at night we stayed at one of the stops for a few hours initially because a mechanic was struggling to fix the air conditioning. I was glad it broke down because it was pumping out such cold air that I had been freezing.

Unfortunately, he fixed it. Then a pretty woman aged about thirty started to cry and swoon with the pain from her false leg. People gathered around her clucking and trying to help. They carried her off the bus. Half an hour later she was helped back on the bus, now quiet, and we were soon on our way.

Arrived at Murajipe at half seven in the morning. The driver said we would not arrive in Salvador for another nine hours! It didn't look as if I was going to get the daytime sleep I was hoping for.

Crossed into Bahia State. The landscape dry, arid scrub, the trees look different. A large village sat on top of hillock on top of which was a huge wooden cross with a Christ figure nailed to it. I felt sickened and wouldn't have wanted to look every day at a man tortured. There was an electricity plant nearby. Perhaps the cross was protection against it. If you are going to have a symbol then why couldn't they use more gentle symbols of Christ healing or praying rather than being killed? I don't know. St Francis of Assisi would be a good model for Christ statues or carvings.

Mile after mile of charred hillsides. Just a few tall cactuses grow on the grey hills. A twelve foot cactus stands sentry near a small white house. Where the hills are cleared and burned I could see where the rain pours down with no vegetation to drink the water or slow and break its path. Gullies form deep into the orange soil of the parched land. Suddenly, the sight of a rare river with people paddling in the shallows.

Many places are heavily littered especially with plastic bags and bottles. They get caught on the cactus, against trees and shrubs, float in the sea, even being carried to this coast from other countries, they are in rivers, they are stacked by the wind on the roadside and blow about in the streets.

Eat lunch at a stop at Milagres. I hoped we might arrive

at Salvador at one o'clock in the afternoon but I was soon disabused of this notion by a passenger, who said arrival would not be until about three o'clock.

Arrived in Salvador at five o'clock after travelling for thirty six hours. I had a super room in a hotel high up with a small balcony and all windows facing the ocean. There are many rocks along this stretch of coast with small rock pools where I see dozens of people of all ages paddling and playing.

Sitting outside on a rock I write a two page letter to my sister who works full time in the north of England. Oops, the wind is strong and it whips away the letter high into the sky and drops it into the sea. This is the second loss of the day because earlier I walked to a local deli to buy water and orange juice. I put a fifty reos note in my bra so that I don't have to carry a purse because of muggers. I walked along humming glad to be in such a great place on a sunny day. Got to the shop and put the goods on the counter – no money. The note had dropped out of my bra. I was now short of money. I retraced my steps but it wasn't there. Passing another small hotel I noticed the doorman watching me. I went and asked if he had found my money. He said no yet the look on his face suggested otherwise. There was nothing I could do about it. It might be of more good to him than it was to me.

The next day I phone to my mum who tells me dad had his op on Friday. He lost three pints of blood beside a bit of his inside and seems, apart from feeling nauseous, to have come through all right. I hope he had a good surgeon. The hospital is in an average area and I worry that he might not get the best treatment because it is not a centre for excellence. He has been in hospital for ten days now and will be very keen to get out and go home. I phone my sister, Ros, and ask about Dad. Ros is reassuring and tells me he is making a good recovery that he looks well and is cheerful. Everyone else in the family is well. It feels odd to be so far away from family when one of them is in hospital. It's the first time anyone in my family has been in hospital for over ten years so it feels strange.

Bahia State is in the north east of Brazil and it the most historic state. Salvador is the state capital. It was the capital of Brazil from 1549 until 1763 in the days when it was the centre for sugar. Italian navigator, Amerigo Vespucci, sailed into the bay and named it Bay of All Saints.

Brazil still farms cattle, and produces gold, diamonds, sugar and tobacco. Economically it is growing with increased food production, exports of cars and minerals from its mines. Almost one fifth of the population in Brazil have no formal schooling and illiteracy rates, especially in the north, are exceedingly high.

Although Brazil has a population of over one hundred and sixty million it doesn't feel crowded once you are out of the larger cities. One of the issues it will have to deal with, as will every country, is population control. Birth control and sex education are not easily available. One of the limiting factors is that over three quarters of the population are Catholic and unless the church starts to promote sex education and birth control the women and society will suffer and poverty will grow. It is ridiculous that women, the sex that give birth, are dictated to by men. Men - who do not suffer the pain or trauma of terminating pregnancy or undergoing dangerous birth. Yet in some countries they remove a woman's right to choose what happens to her own body.

The Amazonian area is 42% of the country. The National Cancer Institute has identified two thousand plants which could hold the key to being effective against cancer. Those plants, in the tropical rain forest, need more testing so that the strongest and best formulas may be developed.

Cashew fruit, a single nut extending from each fruit

The equatorial region was never buried under the glacial destruction of an ice age so that species exist there that do not exist anywhere else.

The town of Salvador is north of Brazil's largest bay, the Bay of All Saints or the Baia de Todos Santos. African music, food and religion still infuse the area.

Breakfast time is like being in Alice in Wonderland. The fruit juice drinks include umba (a type of plum) acerola (cherry flavour with a high vitamin C content), abacaxi (pineapple), caju (cashew) which tastes tart with a memory of something between a lemon and a pear, carambola (star fruit), limao (lemon), mamao (papaya), maracuja (passion fruit) and manga (mango). The fruits are delicious and often made into ice cream or sorbet.

Exploring the old, upper part of the city the architecture is Portuguese in style from the 1600s to 1800s. In the Upper City is the historic centre where the Portuguese starting building in 1549. It has handicraft shops and cultural centre. The Jorge Amado Museum was the old slave auction site in the Pelourinho area. Pelourinho means whipping post and it was here that slaves were whipped and sold until slavery was made illegal in 1835. As with many cities in South America the level of theft crime is high and the short explosive sound of firecrackers going off in the dark night is common.

I walked about the Catedral Basilica one of the older churches built of pale marble between 1657 and 1672. It is the Cathedral of Bahia and was the centre for Jesuits until they were expelled from Brazil in 1759. The baroque church of St. Francis is too opulent for my comfort. How people can go there and pray I do not know. The chandelier contains 80 kg of silver. Gold leaf covers the arches and altar areas leaving very little of the wall bare. There is a wooden rail containing carvings of naked and pregnant females. The cloisters have blue and white wall tiles. There are over a hundred catholic churches and hundreds of Candomble temples, the latter of West African spiritual tradition. Salvador may not be as famous as Rio and Sao Paulo yet it was the first capital of the country and is its third largest city.

Three days later Plainsong arrives in the marina in Salvador. On Sunday night Francis went to an African religious performance where a dead chicken lay on a doorstep in its own splattered blood as a sacrifice to the gods before guests arrived for the service. The service includes drumbeats and some of the congregation go into a trance.

On Monday we both went to a folklore dance show. The dances included one to the god of fire and thunder; to the god of fisherman for a good harvest; a celebration after the sugar cane harvest; capoeira, martial arts type dance; and then the samba. The brilliant dance troupe are the Bale Folclorico da Bahia formed in 1988 by Walson Botelho and Ninho Reis. They are one of the best black dance companies in the world and their thirty eight troupe members have travelled much of the world with the company.

The next night we went to Pelourinho to the see local bands play. We went with Lyn and Robbie and sat in the main square where people sat at cafes drinking Brahma beer, eating Bahian food and eating peanuts. People were strolling or standing listening and watching the muscians playing loud, upbeat, modern songs. A young man standing with his pretty girlfriend chatted to us. He was a drummer with a band called Olodum who give free concerts on Sundays in that area. We went with them to another square with another band playing where the music was even louder.

Urgently needing to visit the loo I turn down the opportunity to use the portaloos that line the street. The street is steep and the portaloo cabins lean slightly. I ask Francis to accompany me to a bar so I can use the loo inside. The Salvador couple try to dissuade me "Don't go in the bar, not good. Use the portaloo." but the option of using the leaning portaloos seems worse than the bar. Francis and I go into the ground floor bar which is absolutely crammed. A young man pulls us from the doorway to the bar. He is smiling and has a friendly manner. He is talking to us in Portuguese. In his mid-twenties with pale skin, long light brown hair and the look of the habitual criminal in his eye I nevertheless keep walking forward. I am now closer to the loo, only two yards ahead now than to the bar entrance now eight yards behind. I am struggling to ask where the loo is in Portuguese because when I open the door pointed out to me I only see a large empty room. A pretty, dark haired girl in her teens understands what I want and pulls me by the arm into the big room and then into an inner large empty room. This is the lavatory.

The floor is covered in a quarter of an inch of clear-ish liquid. I think a pipe is leaking and then I think it is pee. The room, five feet long and three feet wide has two holes in the ground about two feet apart which are at the opposite end of the room to the locked door. The girl points to a hole in the ground. I look puzzled. She pulls up her skirt, pulls down her knickers and squats and pees over the hole. I laugh and

Beautiful clothes and head dress of a shop assistant, Salvador, Brazil

do the same. She waits for me and we leave together. There is no wash basin or tap.

I meet Francis in the hallway outside the loo and we leave quickly, pushing our way through the crowds. A man grabs Francis's can of beer, he resists even though it means the can is crushed and the beer spills. As this struggle happens I see the criminal looking young man try to rip off Francis's watch while his attention is diverted by the man trying to take his beer. Now Francis's face looks like thunder. He always thinks the best of everyone unless he has strong evidence otherwise.

The watch is dear to him because it was a twenty first birthday gift from his father. He is determined not to lose it. One man pushes him while the other is still trying to pull the watch from his wrist. The wrist band snaps. Francis holds the band and watch itself in his hand. With a strong push and thrust forward he leaves the men behind and we are soon on the street outside.

The girlfriend of the Olodum drummer shakes her finger at me. She is hearing impaired and signs to me and I understand her when she points and nods at the portaloos and then shakes her head and her finger at the bar and I nod in agreement. It had been a mistake of mine to go into the bar thinking it safer than the outside loos. The ones outside, rickety though they might appear are safer and cleaner. The drummer says that is why they are there. So that you do not have to go through crowded bars where thieves are active and they are in the open so everyone can see who goes in and out.

Of all the places in Brazil, Salvador was the most active, lively, musical place of all. Most of its population is descended from West Africans taken there against their will and later assimilated and mixed together with the indigenous and the Portuguese population. African history influences the food, music and dance. There are dance displays most days, many not aimed at tourists but for themselves.Young men showing off their skill at capoeira a mixture of self-defense movements smoothly incorporated into a dance sequence. Large well-known bands play twice a week in spacious squares in the old part of town where hundreds of locals gather.

Beautiful clothes and head dress of a shop assistant

Early on Tuesday we set off for a night on Isle Tinare to the south of Bay of All Saints. We caught a ferry from the port in Salvador to the Island of Itaparica, then took a bus down the island, over a bridge to the mainland to Valenca where we caught a small ferry down the river Una and on to the Atlantic and the small island of Tinare.

Itaparica is lush with small quarries dug into the multi-coloured soil. Most of the soil is red but some of it is white, cream, yellow, grey or brown. In some parts of the island there are rolling hills with grassy fields while in other parts coconut palms and banana trees grow. Itaparica is the largest of the many beautiful islands studding the turquoise sea in this part of the country. It is about twenty miles long and eight miles wide

Valenca is a plain, busy town selling spices and with a lot of young men touting for taxi business from tourists. It is a ten minute walk from the bus to the small ferry point. The boat was simple without cover. A blue bench seat went around the edge of the wooden boat and another seat in the middle forming two square shapes. Coffee was available from flasks and served in small paper cups. The ferry moved steadily between healthy mangroves, a vivid green above the blue-green water and below the clear, cerulean blue sky. The mangroves stood on tiptoe raising their green silk crinoline dresses above the water. Sometimes their thin, pale brown legs showed two or three feet above the river surface.

Once we reached the end of the river and began to cross to the island of Tinare the wind blew a little stronger. Many passengers put on a shirt or wrapped cloth around their shoulders. The village of Morro Sao Paulo gradually appeared ahead. On arrival everyone piled out onto the pontoon and walked up a slope towards a gorgeous golden stone arched gateway leading from the ferry to various villages. To the right was a typical white church with bright blue window and door frames. Palm trees grew everywhere. A kind person pointed to the village where we had a booking for the night. Until two decades earlier, the island had few vehicles. There were no roads just tracks in very deep, very soft golden sand. Wonderful. It was quiet and gentle.

Morro de Soa Paulo has several beaches, some just yards away and others a one to two hour walk away. Some of the tracks have now been paved to increase tourism. There are party towns on the mainland further south including Porto Seguro, Arraial de'Ajuda and Trancoso. Morro Sao Paulo on Tinare was a delight. This is wonderfully idyllic if you like quiet, unspoilt places. The few small streets there are made of deep soft sand. There are no vehicles apart from for rubbish collection. Supplies are transported from the small quay by donkey. It is an island for tourists. The hotels and guest houses are generally small, clean and pretty; the beaches unspoilt and the sea clean. A place it is very easy to enjoy eating papaya, locally caught fish and sipping caipirinhas in the warm evening.

Back in the town of Salvador a man is setting the cobbles into patterns on the pavement. There are no mistakes in the miles of cobblestones. I noticed this in Rio too and have seen it in Portugal. Dark stones are laid to make a design in the paler stones. On the edge of the pavement a woman in a long white dress and bright turban is cooking food for sale in a huge metal pan. A man wearing skimpy swimming trunks, keys attached to the top is standing talking in a telephone kiosk that looks like a silver tall wizard's hat. There are also kiosks shaped like a cashew which are white with red and orange edging and yet more the same shape though with colours of red, orange, yellow, black, white, blue and green in stripes. Even the posts they are on are multi-coloured stripes. I smile at the joy of Salvador. Salvador is musical, merry and the most African Brazilian State. Rio, Bahia and Amazonas must be God's Cradle of the world.

Brazil is the exotic flower of the Americas. During my time living in Brazil I found it one of the most dynamic and uplifting of countries. This jazzy, dancy, exuberant place of music and football; where the cool mists blow across the southern states and hot air circles around the north; precious rocks lie in the middle and the Earth's biggest natural plant pharmacy grows in the Amazon region. It is a place to stand back and admire – then join right in…

PAPAYA WITH SUGAR

Epilogue

The South Pacific: In February, 2016 President Francois Hollande of France visited French Polynesia. He admitted that the nuclear tests done had harmed the environment, the islands and the people. He is reported as saying "I recognise that the nuclear tests conducted between 1966 and 1996 in French Polynesia had an environmental impact, and caused health consequences."

The 193 atomic tests took place in the Tuamotu Islands on the islands of Morurao and Fangataufa which have remained out of bounds. The President announced that the government would pay towards Tahiti's cancer-treatment service and declared that a regional grant, known as the "nuclear debt", would be pegged at 90 million euros from 2017 onwards. It was worth 84 million euros in 2016.

South American countries still suffer destablisation by right wing groups without a moral compass.

Art: In 2015 a painting done in 1892 by Paul Gauguin was called "When Will You Marry" (Nafea Faa Ipoipo) was sold for almost £200 million to the Qatar Museum. It was one of his earliest paintings done in the South Pacific.

Computers and smartphones are making astronomy much more understandable because you can either put in the compass co-ordinates or point the phone to the zone in the sky and it will tell you the stars.

Technical Details

Plainsong is a 35 foot ocean cruiser known as a Tradewind.
Weighed 9 ½ tons and built in Salcombe, Devon, England.
Fibreglass hull with teak exterior and American oak interior.
Non slip deck material known as Treadmaster.
Engine was a Perkins, the same as Volvo.
3 sails, Yankee, main and working jib
Self steering gear included both a wind vane and auto-pilot.
Radio : local for calling VHR and SSB for longer distance.
Radar reflector.
2 water tanks : one of 60 gallons and one of 20 gallons
Propane fuel : 40 gallons plus 10 gallons strapped to deck.

Place Co-ordinates

Nuka Hiva 8.8 degrees south and 140.1 west
Ahe 14.4 degrees south and 146.2 west
Tahiti 17.6 degrees south and 149 west
Ushuaia 54, 8 degrees south and 68.3 west
Rio 22.9 degrees south and 43.1 west
Salvador 13 degrees south and 38.5 west

This adventure took place between 1997 and 1999
Several names have been changed to keep their privacy.

AE©

ALICE EVES

Acknowledgements

Thanks to Barbara Beaumont, Justine Gillie and Douglas Addison
for reading the draft

Thanks to Mari and Rodger Martin who suggested and persuaded me
to write about my adventures and also to Christine Hammacott
of The Art of Communication whose terrific technical
and creative abilities have helped to bring this book to you.

To the Tahiti Tourist information office;

Alex B.

www.GranCanaria.info and Bananalink on bananas

statistica.com

The National Security Achive
at the George Washington University, USA

as well as Wikipedia.

PAPAYA WITH SUGAR

ALICE EVES

EXTRA STORY

No Star to Sail By

PAPAYA WITH SUGAR

29th July

A friend and I chartered a sailboat in Alaska to see more of nature and less of people.

The wind was light; the clouds were low as we sailed out of the harbour at Sitka in the panhandle of South East Alaska. It was my first time in the cold air 56 degrees north of the equator.

Sitka is a small town with tall mountains and an extinct volcano around its edges. It is a tough place to live in this harsh, wet, environment where self-sufficient hardy types drive by in rusty trucks and build their own homes.

There are colourful, wooden totem poles in the parks made by the indigenous people, the Tlingit who still live in the area. Sitka was settled by the Russians in the late 1700s, building the town, calling it New Archangel, and trading otter and seal fur. What a deal for the USA when the U.S. Government bought Alaska in 1867! They moved the capital from Sitka to Juneau and let the town dwindle in its commercial activities.

St. Michael's church is a good example of Russian architectural design with its onion shaped domes. It was first built in 1848 then rebuilt later keeping the same design. The area is surrounded by the seventeen million acre Tongass National Forest.

Sailing in a tiny breath of wind we skimmed out of the bay and headed to Beehive Island. The boat, Miiska, was a Yankee 30, fibreglass yacht based in Sitka with a self-furling jib. Before this I'd always had to furl it by hand and it was hard work. The air was cool against our cheeks and smelled sweet and fresh from the pine trees. We wore our life jackets and harnesses were clipped on. What wind there was dropped so we motored for most of the day to our overnight anchorage.

All our food stores had been bought and brought on board in Sitka. I cooked some chicken, potatoes and carrots all in one saucepan with a tasty stock and that warmed us up.

The sea was calm so we slept well. The following morning we set off for Sinbad Point at the entrance to Sergius Narrows. This rather frightened me because I'd read that the water rushes through the narrows at approximately nine knots an hour and our boat only goes at a top speed of five knots, less if sailing in a light wind. This meant we had to get the time and tide right and only go through at slack water and preferably at high slack. Once away from the area the current is much less strong at one and a half to two and a half knots. Going through Peril Strait we had to keep an eye on land features and the compass because there is possible magnetic variation in places of up to four degrees.

Sergius Narrows is a part of the fifty mile long Peril Straight, which has an area Poison Cove, and another called Deadman's Reach. All these names were making me uneasy. Long ago over a hundred men had died after eating poison shellfish so that explained one or more of the names. There is a dredged channel of twenty four feet deep and four hundred and fifty feet wide through the Narrows marked by buoys. It is best to slow down upon approach and be at the entrance at least half an hour before predicted slack water to be ready for local condition variations when slack may be earlier or later.

Bear Bay and Deep Bay are good places to anchor nearby. The latter gives better protection. You can anchor in ten to twelve fathoms in sticky mud. The US Pilot book gives excellent directions and information.

When we arrived at the Narrows half a dozen boats of various sizes were waiting for the right time to travel on. As we went through we saw that buoys or lights marked most of the serious dangers. The speed of the tide and the ferocious winds I knew could hit the area were not appealing. We went through the Narrows confident yet watchful and all was well.

After three hours of sailing my friend Francis spotted a

tail a couple of miles ahead of us.

For now the wind had gone and in the still water heaven on earth put on a show.

Francis was sitting in the cockpit looking forward to our left, the port side. I was at the helm looking ahead and then at the compass course. I looked to where Francis pointed. "Look, look," he said excitedly. "I don't know what it is but it might be a whale."

Sitka by Douglas Addison

Above the glassy sea a plume of what appeared to be water sprayed into the air for eight feet. Then we saw a fin and then that disappeared and we saw a large dark tail lift out of the water and vanish as the whale dived. We watched as the whale did this three times heading away from us and then we saw it no more. It seemed to be a Minke whale judging by its small dorsal fin and body size around twenty five feet. It was almost the same length as our thirty foot boat. An hour later we watched a larger, athletic whale jump and twirl out of the water. Our first sighting of a humpback. We grinned for the rest of the day.

Sheer mountains with tops covered in a thick soup of cloud stood as sentries on both sides of the strait. Ahead and around each bend the views were short and only showed up to three hundred feet of mountain. We spotted two plump sea otters floating on their backs and eventually learned to see the bald eagles high in the trees. As our eyes got accustomed to the dark green trees, the brown trunks and branches and the white cloud we began to notice large, strong, bald eagles camouflaged, their brown bodies blending with the branches and trunk. The head like the snow that falls so much of the year. Each eagle with a territory of its own, solitary and alert. One stood boldly on top of a green buoy.

"Look, look" we shouted to each other pointing as we spotted another one. "What's that?" I asked as water splashed around us. Francis looked. "I can't believe it. The salmon are jumping out of the water!" Every so often one jumped seemingly for the fun of it and back it plopped. We laughed with amusement and joy. The salmon were jumping so close around the boat that I thought if we reached out with a butterfly net we would have caught one.

Sitka is on Baronof Island. The island is called Shee by the Tlingit, which has only a few very small towns and some hot springs. It measures approximately 85 miles by 25 miles with a population of around 8,500. We kept away from the west side of the island, which is pummelled by gales most of the winter and frequently in summer. Brown bears otherwise known as Grizzly bears live here and on other nearby islands as do Sitka deer. The island is named after Alexander Baronof who was a Russian and one of the first to settle and trade from it. The main industries are fishing and processing. There are now even salmon hatcheries here. One of the highest mountains is over 5,000 feet and has the simple name of peak. Another is mount Katlian which is 4,300 feet. Visitors should dress warmly and in waterproofs because the average rainfall in a year is 86 inches and the average snowfall is 39 inches. From October to May snow is frequent.

In Sitka Sound the currents are weak and generally clockwise though they are stronger among the islands. Enforced speed restrictions apply of 3 knots in the small craft basins and 5 knots in the main harbour. The harbour master can be contacted on channel 16.

Sitka Sound entrance is between Biorka Island and Cape Edgecumbe. From the Sound we would head, over an eight day period, to Olga Strait, through Peril Strait to Chatham Strait and on to Glacier Bay.

There are reefs and shoals all over the place to you must use charts and keep a good look out. In Sitka harbour there are three channels. The eastern channel is the main entrance and is the widest. (See charts 17320, 17324-7)

Advice is given to sailors that they
1. Must use oil absorbants;
2. Use spill proof system for fuel;
3. No grey water discharge in marina or within 3 miles of shore;
4. It is illegal to discharge untreated sewage within a 3 mile limit. Must use pump out stations; and
5. Stow it; don't throw it.

In the late afternoon sipping tea and eating biscuits on deck we noticed a patch of kelp to our right about a hundred yards long. In amongst it were two sea otters lying on their backs eating clams. It was a terrific sight at the end of our day's sail. Cold but happy we went put away the sails, tidied up the deck and went below for supper.

30th July
Set off at eight o'clock on a cool, grey morning with low cloud.

It began to rain an hour later. The mountains were so high that it was difficult to pick up a signal to receive the weather forecast. Francis wasn't bothered but I was because I didn't want us to recklessly sail into a storm. A medium sized motor cruiser began to pass us and I recognised "Ocean Lady" a boat that had been on the dock near us in Sitka. We spoke on radio telephone and Brian, the captain, said the forecast was the same as for yesterday.

We passed through the glorious circular Hanus Bay. The water was still and we hoped for whales but didn't see any. We sailed on to the next bay where we would spend the night. Just as we approached we saw three humpback whales blow, jump out of the water, which we later learned, was referred to as breaching, and then flicked their gigantic tails. It was difficult to find words to express the magic. It filled me with awe at their staggering beauty and playfulness.

They are exciting and frightening. Frightening because they are so powerful and large. They can swim at forty miles an hour so much faster than our boat and can grow to fifty feet. It was so beautiful that it seemed every person and every nation in the world should respect and protect these wonderful creatures.

31st July
Got up at half seven and underway at half eight heading for Tenakee Springs. A cold, grey morning with a light wind. A little while later I spotted two whales some way ahead. Reaching for the binoculars I had a closer look and screamed. What I had thought were two whales jumping out of the water together was one huge whale opening his mouth after scooping up a mouthful of fish. Each jaw, top and bottom measured about six foot. Francis looked through the binoculars and saw the whale take another mouthful. We were dumbstruck. Francis was excited and kept saying,

"Let's go up to it. Let's get close and see it." I was hesitant. The story of Jonah and the whale came to mind. I wanted to understand these creatures a bit more before I was willing to sail up to or into its mouth and be gobbled up. We didn't go any closer. Which as it turns out was a good thing. It is fine to let the whale come to you but this is its territory and its best not to hunt it or follow it but to let the creature be.

Before long we turned into Tenakee Inlet on the west side of Chatham Strait. It would be about thirty miles, so a six to seven hour sail or motor if no wind to the small village. It was coming up to four o'clock when we saw a row of ramshackle wooden buildings along Tenakee inlet. They didn't look used. There were about twenty small houses of various sizes built on stilts along the waters edge. This surprisingly was the hub of Tenakee Springs.

We went alongside a small narrow jetty for fresh water where marine fuel was also available and then went onto a pontoon were we tied up the boat for the night. The bottom is hard gravel and shell.

Francis suggested I went to get any food of interest in the small village shop. I must buy baked beans, he said. They are quick and easy to heat up and go with most things. The guide book had said there was a small shop about ten minutes walk through the woods.

"Come with me," I said. "The book says bears live on this island. I don't want to go on my own."

"You'll be all right. Look, I'm going to check and clean the engine then check the sails. You do the shopping." Then he lifted up part of the floor and stuck his head down towards the engine and that was the end of that conversation.

Walking down the wooden jetty I passed a pale, scrawny teenager looking furtive. We said "hello". His glance was quick and awkward.

The narrow path followed the curves of the waterline.

Long grass and wild flowers grew on the seaside of the path. White and purple anemones grew near purple erigeron and blue aconitum. On the other side woodland grew high and dark. My breathing threw puffs of white moisture and my feet crunched and echoed as twigs snapped beneath my yellow wellingtons. I'd read that bears often range fifteen or twenty miles for food. Francis said they wouldn't be on this part of the island but I wasn't so sure. It was a small island and this was their home. They would wander about wherever they liked looking for berries and other food. Kodiak bears can grow over nine feet tall and weigh up to one thousand and four hundred pounds.

Bears don't like noise so I decided to sing. They like to keep away from humans, and I don't blame them. I sang "Summertime". I sang out loudly. My walking speeded up and so did my singing. I started to run out of breath so that the sound of the melody began to be halting with breaks between every two or three words, then the melody disintegrated and I was wide-eyed clapping my hands from time to time and pushing words out into the crowd of trees.

There was a clearing ahead and through it I saw the village just a twenty second walk ahead. Nearly there. I walked on to the bath house and looked at the hours it opened. It was open twice in the day and there were women's hours and men's time. At the shop I got fruit juice, beans and potatoes. "How far away are the bears from here usually?" I asked. "How far away? Well they go about the whole island. They don't usually come into the village in the daylight. They're probably a couple of miles away," the female shopkeeper told me. Yikes.

On the way back with the shopping I sang even more loudly and unfortunately for the bear, out of tune.

Back on the boat Francis said we would have to leave at four in the morning.

"What?" I said.

"Yes. A young lad came over when you were at the shop and he said we would have to be out of the inlet by five so we would need to leave at four because they cordon off this part of the bay with ropes and no one can get in or out all day until the following day."

"Don't be daft," I said.

"No, really. We have to get up and ready at four o'clock and be down there a couple of miles by five o'clock."

"There's nothing about this in the pilot or guide. If it was true it would be in there."

"It might be new."

"Don't be silly. They can't just block off the sea whenever they want."

"I'm telling you we have to go."

"Who was this guy?"

"I don't know. Just a local. He was about eighteen. We chatted for a few minutes he wanted to know where we were from and where we were going and then he warned me about being locked in by the ropes. They are put up by the fisherman. He said to be safe we should leave at four."

"He's playing a joke" I said, "to have a laugh when we are out there in the middle of the night in the freezing cold." I thought it was the thin youth I'd seen earlier.

"Why would he do that?"

"To tell his mates and they'd all think its hilarious"

"He was just a nice young lad. Why would he lie? I think we should go."

"No way. Look we have the cruising guides. They have the most up to date information on where we can anchor, tie up on pontoons, buy food, where the rocks and shoals are and you can be sure that if an inlet was going to be closed off they would let sailors know that."

"But he said"

By now I was sure the idea was preposterous. Kind, trusting Francis had been had.

"Yes, because he's a joker. This is Alaska. It's full of really hardy men and women who are strong and self-sufficient. It also has a few people who come to find themselves and many more who come to lose themselves so that they cannot be found. We have read that a few fugitives from justice come to Alaska. Look you know about boats and I know about people.

I've no intention of leaving in the middle of the night because of what you have been told. We've sailed in the middle of the night because of unsafe anchorages or because of tides and that is fine. I'm not doing it for some cock and bull story. If I'm wrong and we are locked in tomorrow then I'll eat my words and the next time I'll hold my tongue."

That evening we went to the bath house. The hot mineral springs bath house was built for the villagers because decades earlier most of the houses had no shower or bath facilities. Some still didn't. It was also open to the few members of the public who visited the island.

That evening the time for women was 6 pm until 10 pm and for men from 10 pm until 9 am so we went at half past nine so that we could wait for each other outside at either side of ten o'clock.

Benches lined the cream coloured changing room. There was a central bench and a clothes hanging section over it. Instructions said to change in this room, then go into the bathing room. It was important to wash and rinse in that room before getting into the spring bath.

Gingerly entering the bath house it was very dark. The bulb had gone so just a little yellow'ish eerie glow came into the room from the window in the roof. The room measured about twelve feet by twelve and the spring bath about eight feet by four. My nose wrinkled at the strong smell of sulphur.

Taking hold of the dark, damp handrail I went down six stony, slimy, pebbley steps to the floor. There was a large, empty gallon bleach bottle with the top cut off which was to be used for rinsing your body. I splashed some of the water over me then washed and following the instructions, began scooping up the hot spring water in the container and pouring it over me. The water and soapy suds drained away along a sloping and ridged floor.

It felt good. Then I slowly stepped down into the steamy mineral bath. It was glorious. There in that dark, sulphurous bath I saw how humans had bathed for thousands of years. It was a primeval place. I thought how over all time hot springs had warmed tired and cold limbs and rejuvenated people. The smell became less noticeable and the room now seemed pleasant. It was natural and uplifting. After a few minutes it was time to go. It was coming up to men's time.

At the reasonable time of seven o'clock the next morning we set off down the inland towards Glacier Bay. All was peaceful and there were no ropes. Most days had been still so we had motored for many hours. This morning there was a cold, strong wind and rain as we headed for Chatham Strait. The forecast for the day and the one following was heavy rain and gales. Francis wanted to beat the gale and get as far north as we could to get inside Glacier Bay.

By the time we reached the end of Tenakee Inlet I was frozen to the core and the wind was strengthening. I wanted to turn back because I didn't want to be caught in a gale with no safe anchorage within ten minutes. But if we didn't get to Glacier Bay then we wouldn't see it at all because we would have to sit out the gale for a couple of days and then we wouldn't have time to get to the Bay and down again to Sitka in time for our flights. We debated the merits. Francis thought the gale wouldn't arrive until the late afternoon by which time we should be in Glacier Bay and in a safe anchorage. Francis got cross and silent and wouldn't talk. We carried on sailing. I knew that for the whole sailing adventure he would keep up the silence if he didn't get his way so with a mixture of laughing and crying at the same time I said "Okay, let's go on."

The conditions were deplorable. After two hours the heavy rain and wind eased and became fitful. Visibility was poor We could see the land at both sides of the channel up to about forty feet but nothing more. Fishing boats whizzed by; buzzing about, engines echoing in the valleys, travelling too fast for waters full of wildlife. After six hours of mainly motoring with a small amount of sailing we anchored in Swanson Harbour. We had been on deck most of that time keeping a look out for obstacles and for sea creatures. I was damp, tired and cold. It felt as if we had sailed for twelve hours. All the time we had sailed here we had not seen the top of any hill or mountain.

Swanson Harbour is simply a small bay with a strong pontoon against which we tied up. There were three other boats there. One, White Trillion II, was British. It was an Oyster 39. The couple on it, David and Rosemary Whitton, had sailed her across the Atlantic, then trucked her across America to Canada. They had emigrated to Canada and then sailed White Trillion II up to Alaska.

After dinner, just before we were going to bed, the Whittons knocked on our hatch and kindly invited us aboard for a drink. Happily we clambered aboard and went the ten steps down below. It was astonishing how big and roomy she was below deck; Not only that, it looked less like a working sailboat and was luxurious.

On the teak table a small squat vase held local pink flowers. On either side of the table the seating was plump and elegant and the cabin was warm. Warm! I'd forgotten what that was because the heater in our cabin fought a tough fight with the freezing air temperature to keep us above freezing. Occasionally our cabin warmed up to 60 degrees farenheit but usually it was about 45 degrees and sometimes 35 because when we were underway for between six and twelve hours a day there was no heating on.

Francis, Rosemary and David had hot coffee followed by a tot of whisky and I purred over a steaming, creamy hot chocolate. Rosemary and David told us about some of their adventures and we told ours and silently and unseen the time vanished until almost two hours later we said shook hands and said our goodnights. Walking the few yards in the still darkness along the pontoon to Miiska we were soon aboard. We were soon fast asleep feeling happier, warmer and drier than when we had first arrived.

The night was freezing. Under my pajamas I wore long johns and a tee shirt made for campers and sailors. Soft woolly socks covered my feet. I wore my red woollen hat because without it my head was so very cold that I couldn't sleep. My North Slope sleeping bag was amazing; so warm it was a good investment. Shaped like an Egyptian Mummy it was wider at the top and tapered slightly towards the feet. It was thick yet light with a shaped extra part for the head, which could be pulled close under the chin and kept the back of the head and neck cosy. It was a new one for this trip and it made me smile just to think about it. So comfortable and warm it was one of my favourite things onboard.

Drips of water falling on to my face woke me in the morning at eight o'clock. Condensation had formed on the window above my bunk and the air was damp because of all the rain. Francis lit the heater and I put the kettle on. At nine o'clock we were off after breakfast.

Yesterday a gale had been forecast for this morning. This morning the forecast showed worsening weather with the gale arriving sometime in the afternoon. We decided to go in that gap between the two patches of bad weather and before the arriving stormy conditions and make it to Glacier Bay. Once there we hoped to be in protected water.

We sailed by hand most of the time but whether it was still or very stormy we began to use the Monitor Wind Vane which was excellent. During the long hours when we did it ourselves by hand I found if I wore gloves they were not so sensitive on the wheel and slipped slightly in the wet. They did keep my hands slightly warmer though. The disadvantage to not wearing gloves was my hands almost froze to the wheel.

Peering through the rain the terrain was only darkly visible on either side of the wide Strait. During the next two hours the freezing rain chilled my bones. Then it stopped and the way ahead was moderately clear for a about mile. It felt as if I had a tight metal band around my head, digging in hard and cold across my forehead. The pain stayed there all day. We had an early lunch of warming tomato soup, bread, butter and crackers then apple, banana and four pieces of chocolate each. We had a hot drink every hour or so during the day and a biscuit or cracker to keep our energy up. Just an hour and a quarter later fog rolled down the side of the channel but our way ahead stayed clear. Dirty grey squalls rushed across the hills buffeting the boat. The wind speed increased, the visibility got worse and the rain turned icy and heavy.

For two hours we sailed in a dark soup. Two reefs went into the mainsail. The wind rushed down the mountains from the west and then north buffeting the boat When there was a lull in the wind we took the mainsail and jib down and motored. A blue and white fishing boat passed us going in the same direction.

What was I doing here? I asked myself as the rain poured off my yellow oilskins. The only colour around was my yellow jacket, hood up over woolly hat, yellow waterproof trousers and yellow sailing boots and Francis's red jacket, trousers and yellow boots. The terrain, the trees and bushes all looked grey and brown in the dismal day. Time to make a hot drink and snack. Taking my hands off the wheel was robotic because they were frozen into position curled over. It was quite miserable and I longed for a warm bed.

Our journey had taken us up Chatham Strait and then we crossed Icy Strait. A good descriptive name because the water from the glaciers runs right into it. We turned into the entrance to Bartlett Cove, Glacier Bay with relief at quarter past three in the afternoon. We made it!

Our permit for arrival was for the following day, Saturday, but because of the bad weather due we arrived a day early. Francis radioed in to ask for permission a day early which was granted. After tying up on the pontoon Miiska's tanks were filled with fuel and water. Then it was time to head for the safety of an anchorage in Fingers Bay for the night.

Smooth, shiny Porpoises and whales frolicked in the water around our boat. They spend summer in Alaska and winter in California and Mexico where they have their young. Heavy freezing rain threw itself down from the heavens limiting visibility. The sea grew rough and it wasn't until half past seven that we anchored in a pretty bay where the wind was less intense. I hit my head hard on a cupboard when I lifted myself up too soon and it ached for half an hour. Francis lit the heater to warm up the cold, damp cabin and that night he cooked supper and I got into my cozy sleeping bag and slowly warmed up.

When the rain was heavy, day or night the boards were put in the companionway to stop the galley, chart area and our bunks from getting soaked.

At night, down below it felt strange at first to be so enclosed. I felt imprisoned. Even sailing off the west coast of Scotland it wasn't often necessary to have all the boards in. On those nights here in Alaska the rain clattered about on the deck like someone running about and with the shore barely visible. On the few dry nights I slept soundly to the sound of waves gurgling softly past the boat as she rocked slowly up and down like a cradle.

It rained heavily all night. By morning the cabin condensation was dripping and I could see my breath. There was a gale warning for all day so no sailing. Cabin heater put on. By the afternoon it had dried out nicely. The sun peeped out for a few minutes in the late morning and the rain and dark clouds cleared. Francis wanted to begin sailing north towards the glaciers. He thought the gale might miss us or be late! This time I vigorously resisted and we stayed put. Within two hours the winds were strong and so was the rain. A storm had arrived. Fortunately our anchorage was snug and safe and so were we. Porpoises played around the boat in the evening.

As the weather raged about us I read about the local area of South East Alaska.

Alaska was sold by the Russians to the USA in 1867 for 7.2 million dollars. That made it a very cheap purchase at about two cents an acre. The US made some very good land deals that century because in 1803 it made the Louisiana Purchase from France of over 800,000 square miles paying about three cents an acre. Alaska now produces around twenty five percent of the oil produced in the USA. It is twice the size of Texas yet has a population of only two thirds of a million.

We saw on the flags and notices the sitka spruce and the wild forget-me-not. It has a gung-ho attitude and pick-up trucks are the most common vehicles yet the western most part of this wild American place is only fifty miles from Russia. For those who are hardy and like remoteness it has the lowest population density in the country at just one person a mile. One has to adjust this because of course people cluster around the towns and villages and there are places it is too difficult to settle. Almost all communities have no roads to places outside the villages and towns because of the mountains and snow. Small planes and boats are the way to get about. There is also no individual income tax.

The next day, Sunday, 4th August, there was a small craft advisory in effect. We knew we couldn't make it in the time available to reach one of the nearest glaciers which was forty miles away, an eight to ten hour sail. We had to leave Bartlett Cove on Tuesday in order to get back to Sitka in time to clean up the boat and leave for our flight home the following day. There was only one thing to do. Head back to Bartlett Cove and book onto an excursion boat for early the following morning visiting the glaciers.

We set off during a clear spell only to find within half an hour the remainder of the bad weather. The wind and tide hurled the boat about and my head ached; whether from banging it a couple of days earlier or from the cold I wasn't sure. The temperature had been in the 40s and 50s during the day and much colder at night.

At a quarter past three, again, we anchored in Bartlett Cove. There was one lodge so we booked in for a shower and dinner. I decided to spend the night in a warm guest room. Francis insisted on staying aboard Miiska so that in the unlikely event she broke free of her mooring he could save her from crashing herself and breaking up on the rocks. He liked the wildness of it so after dinner I went upstairs to a warm room and he rowed across the dark water to his floating adventure.

Woke at five o'clock and day dreamed about staying in a warm bed all day before dressing but I really did want to see glaciers. I'd had a super night in a cozy room and was ready for the day. My headache caused by the cold had gone. Had a delicious breakfast at quarter to six of a large plate of diced fresh peaches and apples, a glass of orange juice followed by hot oatmeal and a plate of toast. At a quarter past six I was leaving the marvellous Annie May Inn in a van to meet Francis and our excursion ship "Spirit of Adventure". By seven o'clock the ship motored towards the inner parts of Glacier Bay.

The bay is on the north side of Icy Strait. Point Gustavus is at the entrance. Although there is a rule that motor vessels must not approach within half a mile of whales, almost all the vessels disregarded this travelling fast and carelessly along the channels everywhere in South East Alaska.

Reid Glacier was the nearest glacier and that was forty miles away. The ship went at 10 miles per hour near the cove and then 20 further away. At north and south Marble Islands we saw beautiful tufted puffins with pale lemon tufts of hair hanging down behind their eyes. Horned puffins came nearby too. They have black marks above their eyes and a definite line on their beak dividing the yellow part from the orange. There were common murre, pigeon guillemot, cormorants, scoters and gulls.

The white and grey Reid Glacier was at the end of an inlet shrouded in mist. It was possible to see a narrow river of icy snow on its route down the mountain to the tide water.

The snowy wall of Lamplugh Glacier was a glorious pale blue. It was an incredible sight, so bright and pure. Further on the Marjorie Glacier is similar. It was enormous. The wall of ice was perhaps two hundred feet high, an unreal seeming pale blue, rather like the blue of the sky on a clear spring day.

They get their blue colour because the ice is so dense that no colours can penetrate or escape except for the colour blue. The white glaciers, such as John Hopkins glacier, often have brown and grey morain, which is the soil carried down the mountain by the ice.

Majorie Glacier and Great Pacific Glacier have joined and form a gigantic wall at the end of the bay. The ship was at least a mile from Majorie when suddenly there was a loud cracking sound that reverberated in the bay. A huge piece of the glacier calved splitting away and crashing like a tall building into the sea. Everyone gave a loud gasp and shout. Shock waves roared across the water rocking our boat. Suddenly it was clear why the boats don't go close. The explosive turbulence and wash can cause waves up to twenty five feet high. It is in such pristine areas of the planet that changes in warming air, warming sea, and pollution are clearly visible.

On the journey back to Bartlett Cove we spotted three enormous fluffy, baby bald eagles sitting in a high nest. They were dark all over, not developing their white head and feathers until they are at least four years old.

A pebble beach had a large brown boulder, that turned its head and looked over its right shoulder at us as we passed. It was a grizzly bear that had been standing on all fours and heard our engine. That evening we enjoyed a large, tasty dinner at the Lodge in the Cove and once back on board Miiska we fell into a deep sleep after a mentally exhausting, fascinating day.

Tuesday 6th August.   Bartlett Cove to Whitestone Harbour

Nine days into the holiday we saw clear sky. A bright, clear morning that stayed fine all day. The sun was shining, the sky was blue and for the first time we were stunned by the view at the end of our anchorage. Beyond the dark, snow speckled mountains near us was the most magnificent, high, pure white mountain range sparkling and luminous in the sunshine. It didn't seem real. I wondered if the highest I could see was Mount Fairweather at 15,250 feet? I understood then its name. I hadn't seen the top of any mountains at all since we had set sail and yet suddenly and unexpectedly this marvellous vision was before me. Nature is so beautiful and something stirred in my soul making me part of the mountains and the sea and I felt protective of this area and all the beauty of the earth.

The air was still and it was sweet from the spruce trees. There were white, black and the tall, straight Sitka spruce as well as hemlock and cedar. We motored towards Icy Strait and into a thick patch of fog. I checked the radar and listened out for any passing cruise ship that might loom too close. Within ten minutes the fog evaporated and the air was once again clear and bright, perfect for spotting whales, I thought.

Behind us I noticed a blow coming from a whale, the expelled air hanging for seconds six feet above the water, then the small fin then the enormous tail fin as it dived.

The sea a mile ahead seemed to be churning. The water looked as if it was boiling. What was it? It was a line of whales, six of them, perhaps a family coming right in our direction down this narrow stretch of water. They all blew into the still air, jumped high out of the water and waved their tail fins. This they did again. There didn't seem enough space for them to go around the side of Miiska. They were fifty yards in front of us. We had our lifejackets and harnesses on so if the boat suffered some turbulence we would be fine. Would the boat survive a bump or crash from one or more whales?

Should we turn the engine off completely so the propeller didn't hurt them but what if they didn't realise we were there because it was quiet. We turned down the engine and left it idling making a gentle clicking under water and pottered slowly along.

I watched the blows, the fin and the tail fins as they got

closer. Each humpback whale weighs about two tons. My hands held on to the grab rail for when we would be buffeted. It gave me quite a fright. It was silent ... no more blows of air, we looked around constantly wondering where they would come up. There they were a hundred yards behind us! They knew we were here. They knew and they didn't want to harm us. They had dived deep without causing even a ripple near us and they and us were safe. Nothing had moved. I was amazed. More than that - I was in awe of their size and their intelligence and their gentle nature. These wonderful creatures should never be hunted or harmed or chased by sightseers or fishermen. I look at them and am in awe. I sang to them "I love you whales, you make the day so bright and when I see you, the world is full of light." If anything was likely to empty an area it would be my singing. Nevertheless I was so joyful that I simply couldn't help it.

At anchor that evening in Whitestone Harbour, a pretty cove with pine covered hillsides. The trees turned a burned orange colour and then purple under the flamingo pink sky of sunset.

Wednesday, 7th August a glorious clear day with the luminous white mountains still in view.

Left at ten o'clock after a leisurely breakfast. Headed for Basket Bay in a light breeze. Didn't make much headway because the wind was fickle. When we did arrive the wind was hitting us right towards the rocks with no protection so we headed out and towards Tenakee Springs. Saw three whales breaching out from still water.

Enjoyed an early bath in the hot springs. The light bulb had been replaced so it no longer appeared ghostly and spooky. Afterwards we met Mr and Mrs Davies who live in the village and have a motor cruiser called "Tenakee Gal". They kindly gave us large, frozen Tenakee venison steaks.

All residents are allowed a set number of deer each year to help control the numbers.

Went to bed about eleven o'clock feeling tired. The holiday has been completely exhausting because the wildlife is so spectacular and keeps coming by so that there is little time to rest.

Half six in the morning listened to the weather forecast. Bad weather on the way. Heavy rain and strong wind was due. Decided to get under way as soon as we could. Left at seven in the cold and rain. There were a few short breaks in the rain though not for long. Then on my favourite point of sail, we broad reached along Deadman's Reach in a force six.

The plan was to anchor in Bear Cove but upon arrival it was clear there was no protection from increasingly strong wind; fearsome gusts; very heavy rain and a heaving sea. We turned around and sailed for another twenty minutes to Deep Bay, which we knew to be a good place and where the Coastal Pilot book recommends as the safest anchorage in the area.

After anchoring I prepared venison stew on the stove. The meal was delicious, filling and warming.

Friday, 9th August. Under way by ten o'clock. Dry, cloudy with short bright spells. Once more we have to go through Peril Strait. Last night we had to avoid the rip tides in the area. They can look smooth but you can see the sea swirling around the edges. The boat was harder to control as we skirted the edge of one and the current pushed hard against us.

Arrived at the Narrows when the tide was still strong so had tea and biscuits in the cockpit until the water was slack. After the narrows we watched a whale frolicking about for an hour as we sailed along under a misty sky and light wind.

Francis decided to pull in the fishing line that had been trailing for an hour and give up on catching something. Just at that moment we saw a salmon had just been hooked. It was almost vertical in the water with its mouth open. It was large, fat and sparkled in the intermittent sunlight. I thought its mouth would fill with water and it would drown. Suddenly, as the hook part of the line was pulled on board there was a twist and the fish escaped, We both looked at each other and said "Thank goodness" with relief.

It is very difficult to kill wildlife anywhere, and here especially so in their very home were we, the humans, are the intruders into their territory. It seems a madness to kill any creatures when it is not necessary and so clear is this when surrounded by them and in awe of them.

An hour later two sea otters rolled about with each other and played in the water. I could see their little furry bodies and faces, their front paws on their chest and their back feet shaped like flippers sticking out of the water. Sometimes they tucked their tail between their back feet so that the tail stuck up in the water. They went to get some food and then one lay back grasping his food on his chest and eating a clam and the other a sea urchin.

A little later White Trillion sailed by and we spoke by radio exchanging information about weather and good anchorages.

Saturday, 10th August, my birthday.
Sailing from Beehive Island to Sitka.

The night had been stormy with a sea swell that made it impossible to sleep. Looking into the cockpit in the middle of the night we saw that much of the rainwater from the deck had poured into it. Francis put on oilskins and wellies and got a bucket. Ten bucketfuls of water were then emptied into the sea. The drainage would need to be improved. Kept an eye on the cockpit and the boat generally until four o'clock in the morning when, at last, the wind and rain eased and we could get some sleep.

There was no wind as we motored towards the inlet for Sitka. I noticed a small, bright sea plane turn from the corner up ahead on the left and head for the centre of the channel. The engine roared. It was perhaps four hundred yards ahead of us, both heading for each other.

We had no sails up because there was no wind and we were motoring. I didn't think the pilot could see us in the narrow channel so I stood on the seat to be more visible as I held the wheel and guided the boat ahead and hoped the pilot would see our bright yellow oilskins and my red hat. Otherwise, I said to Francis, he is going to take off right in our path and head into us.

The plane accelerated and I could hear the engines rev. We gave as much speed as we could to the boat and turned for the marina so that out side view was more visible but she was heavy and sluggish in the water. Suddenly the noise of the plane's engine stopped. They had seen us. We got into the marina safely and the sea plane took off a few minutes later.

(This trip was made some years before the Southern Oceans voyage when there was hardly any GPS or satellite phone use by the general public.)

ABOUT THE AUTHOR

Alice Eves was born in the North West of England. Alice studied law in England and Wales and in California where she was a member of the California Bar Association. She lived and sailed for ten years with her husband in Southern California though her first sailing experiences were in the West of Scotland around Oban and the Isle of Mull. Alice lives on the south coast of England.

PAPAYA WITH SUGAR

Made in the USA
Charleston, SC
29 January 2017